THE

WRITER

EXPERIENCE

❧❧❧❧

DISCOVER HOW YOU CAN TURN YOUR LIFELONG WRITING DREAMS INTO REALITY & UNLOCK YOUR CREATIVE MIND TODAY

ROGER WILLIS

Your Free Gift

As a way of saying thank you for your purchase, I wanted to offer you a free bonus eBook called **5 Incredible Hypnotic Words to Influence Anyone**

Download the free guide here:
https://www.subscribepage.com/b1b5i8

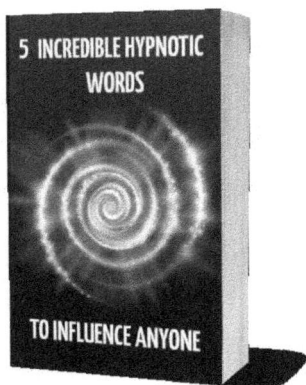

If you're trying to persuade or influence other people, then words are the essential tool you have to master.

As humans, we interact with words, and we shape the way we think through words, we express ourselves through words. Words evoke feelings and can talk to the reader's subconscious.

In this free guide, you'll **discover 5** insanely useful words that you can easily use to start hypnotizing anyone in conversation.

CONTENTS

Write Your Book Today

The Journey to Overcoming Writer's Block

WRITE

YOUR BOOK

TODAY

—————— ❦❧❦❧ ——————

THE MASTER GUIDE TO WRITING A BESTSELLING BOOK THAT READERS CANNOT PUT DOWN

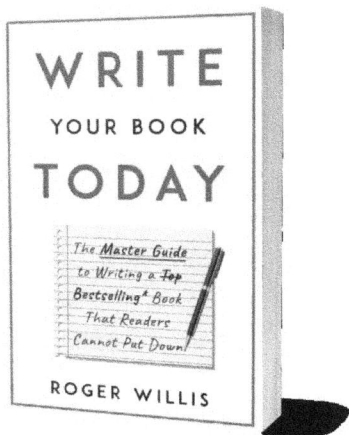

INTRODUCTION

Is there a better way for a smart, busy person to turn their ideas into a book? And how can he or she do it in his or her voice?

That's a question I get a lot. If it's been on your mind too, then you've come to the right place. This book will give you the answer to these questions, but you'll also get step by step guidance on how to get your book done fast.

Almost every entrepreneur in today's world knows the importance of getting a book out there with his or her name on it. It builds credibility, helps you share expertise, and connect with more of the right people. It can also pre-sell your products or services, especially if the content in the book is rich in educational value. The benefits are truly endless when it comes to leveraging a book to build your business or personal brand. Yet most entrepreneurs aren't doing it, and those that do attempt it seem to struggle their way into failure.

Let's be honest. Writing a book is no easy task. I know a lot of intelligent and accomplished people who come to me with great ideas. When I ask them why they haven't published a book yet, the response is usually the same, "I hate writing" or "I just don't have the time or bandwidth to commit to such a laborious task."

1

Both are very reasonable answers, and there was a time when I too, thought the only way to write a book was to commit to the complicated, time-consuming process of traditional writing. As a writer for many years, I am well aware that writing a book is no easy task. The process (whether you call it difficult or not) has always been enjoyable for me. I call it a labor of love. And I understand not everyone is willing to endure that labor just to share their ideas with the world.

The good news is you don't have to use the traditional path. There are better ways you and any other busy entrepreneur can leverage to make sure your wisdom, expertise, and ideas still reach the right people. I even share an effortless technique that you can leverage (thanks to modern technology) to write a book without ever typing a word.

My intention is precisely this for you as I write this book. By the end of this book, you'll finally be in a position to start or even finish your book and feel proud of the final product. But before we jump in, let's talk about your mindset. I want to help you wear the right mindset. Afterall, mindset is everything. The way you approach a project determines whether or not you'll be victorious or fail miserably.

What This Book Is Not

Whether you're doing this as a little fun side project or you want to make sure your startup journey has documented all as you build a successful empire, it's essential to set the right expectations and train yourself into a published author's mindset.

Many entrepreneurs write a book to make some book sales getting some well-deserved recognition as a best seller, and even creating a pathway to speaking gigs. All of these are high expectations to have, but you must realize it will take time to go from a blank page to a bestseller book. Nothing happens in an instant, and you must embrace and enjoy the process. It's also important to recognize the different phases you'll have to go through before you can become successfully published.

This book will help you write a fantastic, high-quality book fast and in an easy to follow style. But you should know, it doesn't teach you how to launch, publish, and market your book. Marketing and selling your book require a different skill set, which I assume you'll work on learning as well.

If you stick with the principles shared in this book, you'll have (in a short while) a book that you can feel proud of as you launch it into the world, whether you choose to create a fiction or non-fiction book.

Since I know most entrepreneurs like to document their journey, share their insights, and tell their story, we will be focusing more on non-fiction writing. However, most of the principles shared can be applied to both fiction and non-fiction writing. And just for your convenience, in one of the chapters, I have included some content to help you with fiction writing as well.

Why People Never Finish Writing Their Book

The New York Times shared a very startling statistic. According to a survey, 81% of Americans feel they have a book in them and would love to write it. Unfortunately, only a few people ever actually get around to writing it.

What's worse is that 97% of writers who start working on a book never finish it. That means only 3% of the people who start working on a book ever get it done successfully. While it is true that writing is a skill set that takes some effort, I think the biggest reason (as with all projects) is the fact that most people come in with the wrong mindset. They lack the persistence, commitment, and focus needed to complete any project successfully. In short, they quit before reaching the finishing line.

The initial burst of excitement wears off even faster than the passionate heat of a new teenage relationship. As things start getting hard, most people abandon ship. I believe this is the main reason why so many half-written books exist in our world. The antidote that can help you avoid this trap is making sure that you keep yourself accountable. When you commit to doing something, take full responsibility, and make sure you see it through.

If you want to join the winners camp, you need to get your head right and create structures around you that support your book goals. Getting into this blindly and in the heat of the moment, just because you've had a great idea, isn't good enough to get you an ideal outcome. The passion has to be there, the knowledge has to be there, and you need to plan for success. Those who do not plan and prepare are setting themselves up for failure. With the right plan and these 20 steps, I will be sharing with you, success becomes inevitable.

Even if you're busy, if you feel like you suck at writing or you're not sure where to start, I know you have what it takes to write and produce a fantastic book quickly. Let's get you to that finish line.

CHAPTER 1

The Fundamentals

Writing a book is such a vast undertaking. It's not uncommon to hear of busy entrepreneurs who sit in front of their computers for 4 hours only to come out of it with three hundred words. Ouch! That's just so deflating.

So, before you sit down to work on your next book, let's learn some fundamentals that have helped me a lot over the years.

Before you can start writing that book, you need to have a thorough plan in place to save you time and avoid the headache that so many writers experience. Your book outline, chapter topics, and the main points you'll cover must be identified long before you start putting the script together. Any research, quotes, stories that need to go into the book must also be presented at this planning phase. The more thorough your plan is, the more enjoyable the process will be as things start to fall into place. To help make this idea more practical, I've outlined some of the critical considerations to make your planning foolproof and have you writing that book fast. For this to work, I need you to clear a large surface on a table or get in front of a whiteboard where you can map out your plan.

How to Write a Book Fast

Begin with the end in mind

I'm sure you've heard this famous line from Stephen Covey's book, and it's very relevant for you in this context. You need to think like a published author right at the beginning of your journey.

Envision what you want to bring out into the world and get as detailed as you can with your vision. How big do you want the book to be? Do you want them to be short, easy to digest chapters, and paragraphs? What looks and feel would you like the book to have? What will be the core message? Here are a few standard guidelines that might help move you in the right direction:

- Ten thousand words can be considered a business whitepaper or a pamphlet. It would take approximately 30 - 60 minutes of reading time.
- Twenty thousand words would be more like a book or manifesto. They would take around 1 - 2 hours to read.
- Forty thousand words would be considered a standard non-fiction book or novella.

These would take approximately 3 - 4 hours to read.

- 60,000 - 80,000 words are long, non-fiction books or a conventional length novel. For this, you would need to allocate a reading time of 4 - 6 hours.
- 80,000 - 100,000 words are biographies, academic books, or epic-length novels. You would probably need 6 - 8 hours of total reading time to go through a book in this category.

As you can see, it's a good idea to figure out which category you want your book to fall into and then do a little math to allocate the necessary time (depending on your schedule).

You must decide on a central idea for your book

Explain what the book is about in one sentence. I don't need it to sound great, and it doesn't even have to make any sense to an outsider as long as you "get it."

It helps if you switch from thinking about yourself to thinking about your reader. For example, if you're teaching something in the book, the main idea can be, "how can I start my own software company with little or no capital?"

Grab your secret ninja tool

What is the secret tool? Post-it notes! I'm serious. Get different post-it notes with a variety of colors and assign each color a specific role. For example, write your central idea on one post-it note and place it at the center of your whiteboard or table (or whatever surface you're using) — the beginning of your planning and creativity. Once we get to chapter six, you'll see how simple it becomes and how quickly things fall into place if you've taken the time to do this.

Block out time

By this, I mean, you must carve out some time for writing. Consistency will make everything more manageable, and it's the fastest way to ensure you finish your book. I know you're busy with lots of things demanding your attention. Emails, text messages, family, friends, clients, and the list goes on and on. Unless you block out time that is only for writing, you'll struggle to get to the finishing line.

Allocate a particular space for writing and a daily word count

I will be sharing with you an alternative hack that can still enable you to write your book fast, even if you feel like you can't type. But assuming you are willing to sit down and do it the traditional way, I want you to set an intention for yourself and choose how many words you will write each day.

It also helps if you find a spot that inspires your creative juices.

Jeff Boggs is a first-time dad with a full-time job as a senior executive in a law firm in New York. When he started working on his first novel, his son was only a few months old. Suffice it to say; his life was full. But he dedicated some time early in the morning while everyone was asleep to his novel. He would wake up an hour or two earlier than usual each morning, grab a coffee, and head down to his basement office to write one page. That's all he did for two years. Now, his book is with a professional editor undergoing final touches before publication. No one should make you feel like you have to dedicate a lot of time and effort into this. As long as you find a way to write consistently and set your daily word-count, you'll build momentum and eventually reach your goal.

Brainstorm

Do it until you find the right idea that hits a sweet spot. Brainstorm what you're passionate about, what you have a piece of in-depth knowledge in, what the market wants, and where these three meets is where you want to write.

11

Mistakes Many Entrepreneur Authors Make

Failing to make a good plan

Remember the crazy statistic I shared about how many writers start but never finish writing a book? That's right; only 3% succeed in reaching their objective. Much of this is because although they have the idea and passion for sharing something meaningful with the world, once they are sitting down in front of a blank page day after day, things start to get tough. Writer's block is a widespread issue, and some people take years to complete their book (if they don't give up before then), mostly because they get stuck.

To avoid this: Make sure you follow the advice I shared above on how to write a book fast. Make your plan as thorough as possible and stick to it.

You are not identifying your category and type of book at the beginning

Again, this takes us back to wearing that "published author" mindset. Your book will most likely flop if you go too broad or try to reach everyone.

You must know what type of book you want to have at the end of this. Is it going to be a how-to book?

Is it a memoir, biography, manifesto, or something entirely different?

To avoid this: Commit to one book type before you start writing.

Failing to test the content and idea before investing a ton of time and effort

We all know a book will require some time and effort, no matter what people tell you. And many entrepreneurs and business leaders feel they have something important to share with the world. So, my recommendation is always to test out the book idea before investing the resources for its creation. There's nothing worse than going through the process and publishing a book only to realize no one cares! Most entrepreneurs forget to use feedback to know if they are working on a great idea. At times, that can be costly.

To avoid this: Use social media to test your insights, find your voice, and even share some of the content ideas you are developing to see how the market responds.

Forgetting to use storytelling

There is power in storytelling, and we are in the era of integrating storytelling into the business. A book is no different. You might have the most impressive ideas, but if you don't know how to keep your audience captivated, the book won't do well.

To avoid this: Incorporate storytelling in your book as much as possible. Share your personal story, tell people about your journey, what that experience was like, and how you felt. You can also use historical accounts or ask your friends and colleagues for permission to use their stories. If you choose to use other people, I do encourage you to protect their privacy by altering some of the private details such as names, etc.

The Difference Between Fiction and Non-Fiction Writing

In simplest terms, the core difference is that with fiction, all the stories originate in the author's imagination. When it comes to non-fiction, however, writing involves real places, people, and stories. It is factual, and, when fabricated, the book loses credibility.

Fiction also tends to be more elaborate and, at times, very whimsical, whereas with non-fiction, the writer sticks to facts and uses a more straightforward approach. Due to the direct and honest nature of non-fiction writing, the core message is pretty visible and can have only one interpretation. As we all know about fiction writing, different readers can interpret the same book in entirely different ways making it a deeply subjective and personal experience.

When writing non-fiction (which is what most entrepreneurs opt for), you must give references for your writing wherever it's needed. For your book to be more credible, it is highly advised that you source your references. The core message of the story must also be identified because, most of the time, people choose to read non-fiction for more than pure entertainment. There is a specific expectation when it comes to non-fiction that it should be informational, educational, or inspirational as well as entertaining. Of course, if you're writing a fiction book, all you have to do is let your imagination run wild, have fun with the writing process and make it as captivating as possible.

In saying this, it doesn't mean that you should stick to writing non-fiction only. You can write fiction books as long as they help enhance the brand you want to build. Many professionals choose to write fiction books because they feel more excited about exploring a more creative and whimsical aspect of themselves. The main thing before you can start working on your book is to decide on whether your book will be in fiction or nonfiction genre.

Getting Yourself Organized

Now that you've committed to writing this book and you know what genre you want to create, you're well on your way to achieving your goal. If you're anything like me, the next logical question is, how do I begin this journey?

There is no simple answer to this because no two authors are alike. Finding your best process will take research, continued experimentation, lots of trials, and error until you hit your perfect sweet spot. The process that works best for you might end up being a combination of different frameworks that you learn from different teachers. You might pick up a couple from this book and integrate that with something you acquired before reading this book and so on. The best advice I can offer is to read, experiment, and repeat more of what works best for you.

Aside from the tips, I shared on how to write fast, I also want to encourage you to reach for the path of least resistance when it comes to getting your writing done. Choose a location that inspires you and enables you to go uninterrupted.

Prep your writing area with all the necessary tools needed, and yes, that includes the colorful post-it notes. Find the right programs and software that help you write distraction-free. Tools like Scrivener and Microsoft are great for writing out your drafts. You also want to choose a simple way of organizing your research so you can easily find what you need. Consider Evernote, Dropbox, and Google Drive for saving your outlines, notes, and research pages. It will make it easier for you if you need to tab between windows to reference something.

If you are writing your book by hand, I still encourage you to create a digital copy of the manuscript using the tools mentioned above. And when it comes to writing tools, here's a list of what I like to use.

Hemingway App:

I write my work on Hemmingway and find it a most pleasant experience. I also use it to test the reading level and simplify my language.

Grammarly App:

I then paste each chapter to my Grammarly during the editing stage. I don't know what I'd do without this tool. It is just incredible when it comes to checking grammar and punctuation, especially if you need a little help with commas!

If you are using the traditional way of writing, i.e., doing it by hand, the tools I would recommend would be a variety of pens, bulletin boards, a writing journal, legal pads, and yes, even then I still want you to use the colorful post-it notes.

Now that you've organized your writing space and have your tools ready, it's time to get to work. Let's brainstorm the main ideas that will help you formulate a book worth reading.

CHAPTER 2

Identifying Your Ideal Reader

Most entrepreneurs fall into the trap of having to come up with an idea, written a book and published it without ever considering whether or not the topic would be of interest to the audience they want to reach. Since I know it's a familiar blind spot for new authors, let me save you some failure here by bringing your attention to the most critical aspect of your writing project: Your ideal reader.

It doesn't matter how great your idea is or how unique your perspective is. It also doesn't matter the length or category of your book. If you don't connect with your ideal reader, all that work will be in vain. To resonate with your perfect audience, you need to know your ideal audience.

Too many entrepreneurs are more in love with their ideas than they are with their customers. That's the old way of doing business, and in today's world, it won't end well. The same is right about your book. Although it's excellent to call yourself a published author and possibly make some money from this project, your primary focus should be captivating your reader. You can only know what will work for your ideal audience if you do some research and get into the mind of your perfect audience.

Identifying your ideal reader is about knowing who they are, where they hang out online and offline, and having a good understanding of the content they find interesting.

You need to know what their needs are, what they are longing for, and what their current state is. The primary purpose of your book should be to help improve the lives of your audience in some way. That's the secret to succeeding at this. So, as you decide on the topic and central theme of the book make sure your ideal audience is at the foreground of your mind.

Quick brainstorming exercise:

Sit quietly and write down on your post-it notes the key ideas you intend to write. You can start with several and drill them down into one or two that get you fired up.

Now that you have one or two potential ideas, it's time to do a little digging and see what genre that idea would fall into, what the current market has around that same topic, and what other successful authors have done. Sites like Amazon are a gold mine for getting these answers quickly.

<u>Try This:</u>

Once you find an author and genre you like, go through every comment (or as many as you can) on the top-performing books from that genre and especially from the author/s you want. Watch out for the response the readers give. Identify the type of readers you would like to have to comment on your book once completed. This becomes a starting point for you, you will see what readers want, what they like, and what they would like to see in the future. You are then able to create something that fills that gap.

Get clear on how your ideal reader thinks. Why would this person purchase your book? What is it about your book that appeals to them?

Create a list of all the benefits the reader will receive as a result of purchasing your book.

How will your audience be able to find your book, and what will be the convincing points that will encourage them to buy once they find you?

This one is optional, but I highly recommend doing it. Once you have an idea, a genre, a title, and an outline ready, take the information gathered from researching your ideal audience and test to see the reader's reaction to your not yet created book. How do you do this? With a little creativity and the magic of Facebook advertising.

You can set up a fan page for your book long before you start writing it. Run a few ads targeting your ideal audience and monitor the reaction. Using free tools like Canva, you can create

21

artworks for your book to help you visually show your reader what they can expect. Not only will this help you generate feedback and even motivate you to write faster. The more robust your idea seems, the higher your chance of success, so you can go all-in with the confidence that you're on the right track. It also helps you grow a fan base for your book long before the publishing date. Talk about being savvy!

Keeping Your Reader Captivated

Whether you're writing fiction or non-fiction, it's vital to grab the attention of your reader and keep them engaged and captivated throughout the book.

Betty Rogers, a literature teacher in middle school, excitedly shared with her friends (during their weekly book club coffee at Starbucks), the mystery and intrigue of a book she'd just finished reading.

The Van Gogh Deception is a fiction book that involves some of the famous artists' works and a mysterious 12-year old boy with Amnesia. "The book has short chapters that are easy to read and was so well scripted that I found it hard to put the book down. When I sat down to read the book, I was planning on going through the first few chapters only. Two hours later, I was still in the same spot turning page after page until my husband came and pulled me out of that mesmerized state. "She couldn't help but chuckle with excitement as she retold the experience to her three book-loving friends. And all the ladies couldn't wait to get their hands on a copy of the book too.

That is the power of knowing how to write a good book. It can keep your reader mesmerized for hours on end. You want your ideal reader to have the same reaction Betty Rogers had.

I'm sure at some point you've read something that enthralled you the whole way through. What was the main secret behind it, you ask? Simple.

The author managed to capture your emotions. You developed an emotional attachment to the character and the unfolding of the story. It's no different than what Hollywood movies do each year to cash in billions of dollars in box office sales.

The fastest way for you to emotionally engage your reader is to create desire and fear within the context of your writing. We all experience a vast range of emotions motivated by our hopes and fears.

When we come across a story with characters that share the same desires and fears that drive us, it naturally draws us into the story, and we "feel" as though we are part of that story. Most of the time, this is a very unconscious experience. We may not consciously know what's drawing us in and making us obsessed with knowing more, but the fact remains: we are in resonance with the emotions portrayed within the story.

Therefore, some of the things you need to know before starting your book include:

Your reader's desires and fears

To do this, I encourage you to dig deep. Dig deep within yourself; dig deep into the main character and the central message of the book.

Tap into your feelings and personality and think of what your audience will resonate with most, which intense emotions will touch them. Self-reflect on the primary emotions you easily identify with then do your best to demonstrate (show don't tell) these strong emotions. Readers want to experience these emotions through action and dialogue, so keep this in mind as you unfold your story. I also encourage you to think about the emotional journey of this book. When will you start building tension and show the "struggle" that the character has to endure? How will you keep that tension going without creating going too far, especially if it's non-fiction? And finally, consider what kind of emotion you want to end with to close your book.

There must be clarity on the emotions that will represent your writing, and at the end of your book, your reader must come out of it feeling a certain way. Take some time to map that out for your book intentionally.

Aside from this very crucial understanding of generating strong emotions, there are a few other things to consider if you want to captivate your audience.

Avoid Jargon and acronyms

Every industry has its language. For new readers who are just discovering you, writing your book using industry jargon is like speaking in tongues! Steer clear of using too many acronyms, especially if you're not planning on explicitly saying what something means. Keep things clear, concise, and easy to understand.

Humanize your writing

It is especially crucial if your book is non-fiction. The more you can put a human face and incorporate storytelling into your text, the easier it will be to create an emotional connection that will capture the reader's attention.

Take time to work on your introduction. If you do a poor job at the beginning of your book, you'll lose! You must work and rework the first few pages of your book to ensure you're giving the reader what they want. The more they feel like you "get their needs" in the first few pages, the longer they'll keep turning those chapters.

Defining Your Niche

In today's world, where everyone is looking to write a book and position themselves as an authority figure and bestseller, you must find a way to make your book stand out. The best way to do this is by choosing a niche that you can focus on solely. And of course, having read this far (assuming you've done the work and know your ideal audience), it shouldn't be too much of a task to identify the niche you'll focus on going forward for your book.

The more you can hone down on a specific niche within your chosen category, the easier it will be to determine the best angle and central focus for the book.

For example, think of the book "The Four-Hour Work Week: Escape the 9-5, Live Anywhere and Join the New Rich" by Tim Ferris. This book attracted its ideal reader in droves. The primary audience was disgruntled, corporate employees. And given the survey findings from Gallup that showed 70% of employees are disengaged from their jobs, I can see why the book was so well received. Since its launch in 2009, the book has been translated into 35 languages.

What you may not know about the success of this book is the "behind-the-scenes" work that Ferris did before publishing. He tested out different titles of the book through Google ads to see which one drove the most traffic. Talk about being a savvy author. So, when we launched the book with this title, he wasn't just guessing, he had data proving that his ideal reader was interested in reading the book.

That alone should inform you of the importance of testing your ideas and leveraging the power of social media even before publishing. The reason I emphasize choosing your niche before writing the book is that it will help direct the actual content you put in. When you know exactly whom you're writing for and what you want them to learn from you, the writing flows more smoothly.

Here are a few questions to start asking yourself if your niche still feels unclear.

- Who can relate to the information I have to share and the story I want to tell?
- Who do I want to inspire/entertain/educate/help?
- Who else do I think has been through or is currently going through a similar experience? What are some of the problems they are facing that my book can help solve?
- Do I already know people or clients that could form a pocket of people I identify as my niche?
- What do I feel passionate about, am I skilled, and knowledgeable in that topic? And where do my passions, knowledge, goals, and audience interest intersect?
- What category do I want my book to base in?
- Where do I want my books to be sold?

CHAPTER 3

Fiction and Non-Fiction Basics

Whether you're writing fiction or non-fiction, I believe the best writing to be one where the reader gets so immersed; they can't wait to delve deeper into the book. With fiction, it can be easy to see how (using fantasy), one can be able to recreate a world that consumes the reader's attention. But I want you to know that even with non-fiction, you can be able to take the reader on a journey that makes them forget they are reading a factual account, leaving them hungry for more.

If you are going to write fiction, here are a few basics to keep in mind.

Fiction allows you to let your imagination run wild. Invent a world that helps your reader escape reality and take them on a journey that will leave them wanting more.

Focus more on scenes and narratives rather than chapters.

It is especially important when working on your first draft. Yes, the first and last chapters are indeed important, but as a fiction writer, the scenes are what determine how captivated your audience will be. If you consider the fact that in a platform like Amazon the first 10% of your book is accessible to your readers so they can decide whether to buy or not, I will encourage you to focus on building up your scenes in such a way that it hooks them from the get-go. The chapters will naturally fall into place when you get to the editing phase.

You've got to master narration and description with your novel writing, as these are the basis for a great book.

Narration is the way a story is told, which includes who is telling the story and the point of view they are using. Is it first person, second person, third person, or a mixture of the three? For example, I am writing this book with you as the main character. That would be considered the second person.

The description is everything, especially for fantasy novels. Think of Harry Potter, The Lord of the Rings and Game of Thrones. These books have done incredibly well because of how detailed and descriptive the author was. As a non-fiction writer, I often struggle with this because I find it hard to be as descriptive as some of these authors. But if you're going to write a fiction book, this is something you'll have to master and enjoy doing. With practice, you'll learn to invoke all the senses and describe the world you're creating vividly. It might take a lot more rewrites than if you were just writing non-fiction, but if you enjoy it, I say go for it!

Since this book's primary focus is non-fiction, simply follow the framework and steps provided in the next two chapters, and you'll have yourself an epic book.

Finding a Creative Paradigm That Works for You

Do you want people to turn that last page of your book, place it back on the shelf and go on with their day talking about the latest trends to their friends? Or do you want to have a Betty Rogers experience where your book is the story of the week they want to share with the world?

All the best speakers, storytellers, and broadcasters in the world know this all too well. Focus on one clear message and have a clear goal in your writing. It is usually encouraged when it comes to speeches and presentations, but it works very well for writing as well. If you have a clear goal, you can find a creative paradigm that works for your book.

It's easy to create something incredible when all you have to do is focus on your "one thing." So, what is your "one thing" going to be in this book?

Going back to the earlier exercise we did where you created a simple statement that will become the central idea of the book, does it align with the "one thing"?

It isn't something you can learn to do in any class, and while it does help to get professional help or some kind of training, you are a unique individual. That means no other writer can do what can do. Every writer is different, and the approach that works for one may not work for another. The one underlying truth, however, is that success is inevitable for any writer who does a good job clarifying their core message and approaching it from a paradigm that authentically resonates with their personality.

That includes the prep work, the environment they work in, the strategy behind their book creation, and the angle of the story they tell. It might be the same topic, but it will certainly not be identical because every author is different. The more you understand your creative paradigm and focus on your "one thing," the more successful this endeavor will become.

Permitting Yourself to Write Badly

If you want to be a great writer, you have to embrace failure and permit yourself to suck! Yes, producing lousy writings will develop the necessary skills needed to make you a masterful writer.

Megan McArdle wrote a book called The Upside of Down, where she pointed out something that has stuck with me. In the book, she had a quote that said, "You can rewrite garbage. You can't rewrite nothing." She also pointed out that students rarely get to see the bad rough drafts behind famous books, but rest assured, there are bad rough drafts.

All writers indeed go through lousy writing to get to the good stuff. The process is just as necessary as the success that comes at the end.

The biggest obstacle you will have to face as you write this book is your own little voice. That voice that keeps correcting you and doubting your ability. The self-conscious tendencies that make you overthink things. Nothing will stand in your way more than fear and a need to be perfect. Fear of failing, fear of judgment, and fear of rejection will keep you from getting to the finishing line, so be wary of these human tendencies as you begin this journey. Realize that the only way to create something remarkable is to practice. Mastery is about practice, and practice is always messy. Just ask a toddler learning to eat or walk or write their name.

One thing I can assure is that every day spent writing is a day where you learn something, improve the skill, and get better at it. Perhaps you'll come up with a better angle or ideas you would have never thought of before. The most important thing is to love the work you do. The process of creating this book, which also includes stumbles along the way, is just part of the journey.

Creating Compelling Characters

We are now in the thick of things, gearing up for a great climax. You know your category type, your niche, your ideal reader, and you already have the right creative paradigm. It's time to start focusing on the book.

Any good book must take the reader on a journey, and as I said earlier, evoking the right emotions is critical. The best way to do this is by establishing the right characters for your book. Fiction and non-fiction books require characters. With fiction books, you'll have to go more in-depth than what I am about to cover here. You'll need to know your characters so well; you could write biographies about them if you wanted to. It takes time and effort.

But for non-fiction, this is all you need:

- Know your characters. That means you need to have a small profile outline with personality traits, emotional disposition, strengths, weaknesses, and insecurities
- Identify the needs, longing, and desire that they have. There should always be a problem that needs solving. Feel free to use Maslow's hierarchy of needs to determine what your character is seeking.
- Build empathy. Characters are always compelling when we can share their struggles and cheer on their victories.

Thinking Through Your Theme

What is the theme? It is the central idea of the story and sums up the book. The statement that you came up with earlier on is the one that we need to develop first before we get into the details of writing your book. We have to make sure it's a good theme that you'll be able to expand throughout the book without getting stuck.

An example of a central idea or theme would be: Love conquers all. He who dares wins.

The central idea of your book will help us find meaning. It is usually a universal truth expressed in your writing. The theme of your book will help keep the flow and direct the reader to your intended outcome. It is usually derived from the emotional development of your book's characters or from the consequences those characters face as a result of their external actions. There are three questions you can ask to test whether you've identified the best theme for this book. Reference the characters you've chosen as you go through this exercise.

- What is the plot/ story of my book?
- What is the meaning behind the story?
- What is the main lesson?
- Who is my character at the beginning of the book?

What are their flaws, and what holds them back from fulfillment or success?

How do the events of my story shape my character for the better or, the worse?

Who has my character become by the end of the story?

For example, you could have chosen to make your theme empowerment, happiness, etc. Take a moment to see how that central idea is encapsulating into the thematic message in your statement.

Here's what I mean: If your primary purpose is "empowerment," then a great comment might be, " You'll never fully come into your power and success by standing in someone else's shadow."

See how simple it can be? Now test it with your central idea.

Integrating this into your writing:

The best way to incorporate your theme is to root it into your main character's flaws or in the obstacle that keeps him or her from reaching their goal. We do this because we want the central idea to unfold naturally as a result of your characters' internal arcs. In other words, as your character changes (or doesn't change) during the unfolding of your story is what will allow your readers to pick up on your story's thematic statement

CHAPTER 4

Ingredients for a

Great Story

One of the best ways to get inspired to create your book and tell your story is to spend some time learning from businesses that are crushing it with their storytelling. Nike is famous for storytelling, and boy do they do it well.

But there is another brand that's captivating hearts all over the world with their storytelling — ever heard of Airbnb?

This brand is proving against all the odds that anyone can win in today's economy. And they are also demonstrating the power of great storytelling. In a captivating Airbnb video called Breaking Down Walls | Wall & Chain, the brand tells of an Airbnb guest called Catherine. She took her father (a Berlin wall guard at the height of the Cold War) on a trip around Berlin. She wanted to show him the vibrant city of Berlin had become. Although the Berlin wall came down, for her father Jörg, the chains and restrictions seem to rule his life still. What makes the story so compelling is the fact that the man who was hosting the Airbnb home she booked was none other than an old friend of Jörg, who also worked as a guard during the Cold War. The video is truly inspiring and helps demonstrate what a great story can do in drawing people in and making them remember your brand. When you use the right storytelling ingredients, you're able to create an emotional connection with your audience immediately and organically pre-sell your brand.

Although this is an example of a video, the same ingredients used in this video, other famous Hollywood movies and books will apply to your book project as well.

Many famous Hollywood producers have known to say that one only needs passion and originality to create a great story, but my experience has shown me there's a little more to it than that. Yes, you want to have a passion for this, and you need to allow your creativity to lead. But it might help if you also add in the following five pillars.

The Five Pillars

If writing a fiction book, here's what you should focus on:

The world vision

In fiction writing, the world where the story takes place needs to be well defined. Which means you need to visualize the world in its minutest details before the novel begins. For example, J.K. Rowling has enjoyed great success with her books because of how well-formed Harry Potter's world is. The readers are fully immersed in his reality as they go through each chapter. It is what you want your readers to experience, as well.

The characters

You must create a detailed character profile for all of your major characters. You need to know your character so well that you can write a biography about them. Make sure you know everything about them even if you don't use all the details in the actual writing.

The plot

The plot, or storyline, is the basis for all actions in the story. It must be engaging. You can have a fantastic world and marvelously defined characters, but if your plot isn't appealing, your readers will get bored. A story isn't limited to one scenario. You can have a variety of plotlines going on for more complex stories, just like Avengers: Infinity War had different plot lines going on for the Guardians of the Galaxy, the Avengers on Earth, Thor, and so on. It directly ties into the events, which are the action scenes that follow the main storyline.

The description and supporting details

It is where your world-building and character profiling comes into play. Give your readers a little context so they can easily follow the story and use description and dialogue to give insight into the main story as well as the characters, how they think, what they desire etc.

The events

The events are the 'scenes' of your story. Every event needs to push the story onwards, following the plot. If they don't, you could leave your readers feeling confused, or the story could seem to drag on without purpose. Events need shaping following your plot. For example, if one of your scenarios is related to family drama, and your characters belong to a family, a good event might be a dramatic family dinner.

If writing non-fiction, focus on these things:

The research

Since non-fiction is based on facts, the more research you put in, the more productive your book will be. Gather your information from credible sources and site back your references.

The character or subject matter

Similar to fiction writing, your book will need to have characters even if the character is the subject matter. The more emotionally attractive your character, the more engaged readers will be. Although you don't have to get as detailed with your characters when writing non-fiction, it's still a good idea to identify their personality traits, flaws, strengths, desires, fears, etc.

The journey of the reader

Every book, including yours, must have a story arc — a trip from the old world to the new Promised Land. Even a simple recipe book will take the reader through the journey of not knowing how to cook something to having a perfectly executed delicious meal. Be intentional about this journey and plot it out.

Story-driven facts and statistics

The more facts, real-world stories, quotes, and examples you can share with your readers, the better. However, I encourage you to be tasteful about this. Instead of filling up the page with dry and dull data, aim for creating stories around the data that help you pass on the same information. Consider including testimonials and case studies if that is relevant to your book. I personally think every business book should include several stories spread across the chapters of the book to help emphasize the main lessons.

The events

How are you going to group, organize, and synthesize the information you've gathered? The flow of the information should make sense to the reader.

Now that you know what to focus on, let's dive deeper into the elements that will help you write a page-turner.

Set the stage

All the world's a stage said, Shakespeare. Your writing needs to do a great job setting the scene and giving your reader context. Otherwise, no connection will be made. A simple way to make sure you set the stage right is to answer the five Ws. Who? What? Where? When? Why?

Sometimes, setting the stage right could mean starting your book right in the middle of something attention-grabbing. Don't be afraid to take a little risk and begin in the middle of it if it makes sense to do so.

Provide a hero worth cheering for (the underdog)

A great story must have a hero that people can champion. Someone the reader can quickly identify and empathize with immediately. When writing non-fiction, make sure the hero isn't your product or service (especially if it's a business book). Assuming you've done your homework well enough to know your audience, this part should come easy.

The other aspect to remember is to make the ultimate goal or desire to make your hero known.

Giving your hero a worthwhile goal makes the story more meaningful. He or she must be seeking something, and they need to be working toward a goal that everyone believes they deserve to have.

Introduce a strong villain

And of course, with any great story that has a great hero, there will always be a worthy opponent keeping our hero from attaining their dream. The nemesis of every good story is just as important as the hero. The "villain" helps us connect with the journey the hero has to go through to attain their goal. The bigger the villain, the better! So, take your time fleshing out and identifying who your audience needs to see as the villain keeping them from having what they desire.

Have a guide and a special gift

It is the point at which whatever you are offering becomes essential. The guide is usually that wise person that steps in when the hero seems too burdened, unable to overcome their struggle. Every great story has a guide both in fiction and non-fiction. You most definitely had a guide that helped you reach your point of transformation. It is how you've been able to translate your past mishaps into an instant success. In many cases, the guide offers some kind of special gift that empowers the hero to transcend current limitations and achieve the desired outcome finally.

If you are writing a business book, this becomes the perfect opportunity for you to position yourself as the guide and offer the "special gift" of your product or service. When people see how your product or service is integral to their success; they will naturally seek your brand out.

The conflict

A story would fall flat if there were no conflict rising between the hero and the villain. If you have watched Captain America: The Winter Soldier, then you no doubt recall the scene where Captain Rogers finally came face to face with the unmasked "Winter Soldier" and how disoriented he was to realize it was his best friend, Bucky. All this time, he was trying to stop this awful villain that was causing so much harm only to discover that if he wanted to stop Hydra and save people, the fight had to be with the only childhood friend he ever had.

The meaning of conflict in your writing is to describe the ongoing struggle of your hero. It will help them reach their goal. The deeper, more twisted, and dark that gap is, the more dramatic the story. I don't know if you know this, but part of why we love stories so much is because we're addicted to that dramatic tension and feeling of suspense.

When we can be able to recreate that feeling in non-fiction, readers won't be able to put the book down.

The famous playwright David Mamet said, "The audience will not tune in to watch information. You wouldn't, and I wouldn't. No one would or will. The audience will only tune in and stay tuned in to watch the drama."

It is right on television, it's evident on social media, and it's what you need to build into your book as well.

Different Types of Conflict

By now, you see the importance of creating conflict and laying it out for the reader as early on as possible. Building conflict in your story is very similar to throwing a pebble into a pond, knowing that it will have a ripple effect that sets cause and effect into motion. As you think over the central conflict in your book, here are a few common types of conflict, many authors and screenwriters use.

Person to person (relational) conflict

It is usually between two characters. In the example I shared above of The Winter Soldier, Captain America (Steve Rogers) came face to face

45

with his best friend Bucky, who was now the main villain standing in his way.

Internal conflict

This type of conflict is well represented over the years in so many brilliant ways. Shakespeare is famous partly since he was able to demonstrate this inner battle so beautifully in his plays. Here, your hero is struggling with his inner world. When a character is unsure, struggling with self-doubt, or dealing with other types of insecurities, a lot of tension is created in the story because his behavior impacts the plot and outcome of the story.

Societal conflict

With this type of conflict, your hero is battling a more extensive system. It can be an organization, a government, a gang, a corporation, or even a country.

Cosmic Conflict

This type of conflict is best created if your hero is dealing with an invisible entity, the devil, a supernatural force, or God.

To create a better conflict, get inside your main character's mind, and see the world from his or her perspective. Making your starting point his point of view will help build the struggle and create obstacles that will stand in the way of him or her reaching the objective. Think about The

Winter Soldier one more time. It would be a little less complicated if Captain America were only fighting Hydra and their infiltration at Shield. But the fact that their "big gun" was his best friend, someone he loved and trusted and the only family he had growing up, made the obstacle much bigger. From his point of view, Bucky was a good man and his friend, yet he was the obstacle standing in the way of saving millions of people.

Remember not to gloss over the struggle of your hero's journey. It is what helps hook the reader and helps them connect to the importance of the transformation that leads to the outcome.

CHAPTER 5

20 Steps to Writing Your Book

It's not enough to assume that because you're excited about writing the book now that you'll be able to see it through.

Step One: Commit to writing, finishing and publishing the book

So many authors never finish the book, because they quit. That's just the harsh truth. Whether it was justifiable or not, the fact of the matter is that they did not see it through to completion.

The best gift you can give yourself is to make the first step toward writing this book a personal commitment to yourself. Complete this binding statement of promise:

I [your name] do vow to myself that I shall write, edit, finish, and publish my book. Through good times and bad times, even if the writer's block comes knocking or the holiday season comes distracting me, I pledge to diligently work

to produce this book and learn as much as I can in the process. I also choose to have fun with this and trust in the journey, knowing that it will make me a better person in the end.

Signed [your signature] on this day [date]

Step Two: Research

Because we are focused on helping you write non-fiction, this has to be one of the first things you do when you start the writing process. The more you can support your facts with credible resources; the more valuable the book will be to your readers. Collect all the evidence needed to support your central idea and then begin the actual writing process.

For example, let's assume I am writing about "how to become a highly paid email marketing specialist."

If I want my book to do well, I need to gather as much information as I can on email marketing. Statistics that show the incredible return on investments for businesses doing it right is a credit to great email marketing, etc. I would also research other experts in my niche and arrange to interview them. There are many companies such as HubSpot and Content Marketing Institute who have carried out extensive research on this topic, and it would do my book well to cite some of the findings shared by these companies. Going deeper into my study and using my own experience as well as credible sources to make my case will ensure my reader buys into the solution I will offer within the book.

Step Three: Don't skip the mind mapping

Once you feel like you've gathered enough of the information, you will need to write this book; it's time to mind map your book so you can see the finished book.

Start with the idea. Then write your one-sentence summary of the book. Expand that sentence into a full paragraph. Take that single sentence and give it some meat. Make sure everything that goes into this helps the plot unfold.

Write down whatever comes to mind. Don't stop yourself. It is where you must allow yourself to essentially "brain dump." Everything that's going through your head around this idea deserves to be jotted down even if you won't use it in the book. Remember the simple post-it note tools that I mentioned earlier in this book? It would be a great time to use them. Randomly add any ideas on those little notes, they may come in handy later. Don't worry about making sense or being organized.

Allow your creative juices to flow and think of as many ideas around your given topic as you can.

Step Four: Write down the main problem, the solution to that problem, and how to implement the solution

This step is where being a non-fiction writer differs from fiction writing. Instead of focusing so much on the scenes, events, and descriptions, we must focus more on the problem, the solution to the challenge, and ways of implementing that solution. The journey from the issue to the solution becomes our primary focus, and your book will naturally divide itself into these three main parts if you follow this formula. It also makes it easier for the reader to stay in the flow of the book.

Step Five: Get clear on your style, tone, and format the book will take

If you are writing a "how-to" book, your book should follow the format that's proven to deliver the best results. For example, I can write my "how-to" book on email marketing using the following formula.

Introduction
Step 1
Step 2
Step 3
Step 4
Step...
Conclusion

If you're going for thought leadership or memoir, these types of books are a bit more complicated to create formulas for, but I still want you to create some flow and structure around it. You also need to determine the tone of your writing and decide whether you'll be formal or informal. Will you use humor, sarcasm, etc.?

Step Six: Define your significant characters or the stories you want to include in the book that supports the unfolding of the solution

With non-fiction, you still want your book to have some characters. Even if the villain is a force of nature, an organization, or an object, it always makes sense to give human qualities and emotions to these characters. It is also where you start identifying the main stories, examples, quotes, testimonials, or anecdotes the book will include.

Step Seven: Group your ideas

Now that you have so much information randomly piled up on your desk, whiteboard, or wherever you choose to do this, it's time to organize the stuff you've written down. Create a hierarchy and start to see chapters and subchapters. It is where the book begins to take form. Things of a similar nature need to pairing together.

Step Eight: Develop a table of contents and summary chapters

If you group your ideas properly, this next step will naturally follow. The various sections that you've now created with the post-it notes can easily direct the table of contents. You want to take the main idea around the groups and make that the chapter. The other thing I recommend is writing summaries for each section before moving on to the next step, and I will explain why in the next step.

Step Nine: Take the different sentences or ideas you wrote down and expand on them into a full-page

At this point, you have lots of different ideas grouped and chapter outlines as well. It's time to go back to the central idea to check and make sure the chapters align with that central theme. You need to stay on track and not deviate; otherwise, this will dilute the strength of the plot.

Now, remember, I suggested creating a summary for each chapter? Here's why. Once you confirm that your central idea is in alignment with your chapter summaries, you can quickly start expanding these short sentences into a full page. From there, it's just a matter of actually sitting down with your chosen tool and turning each page into complete chapters with compelling stories, solutions, anecdotes, statistics, etc.

Step Ten: Set S.M.A.R.T weekly goals and the publishing date for the book if you're self-publishing or the date you will send it out to your agent.

If you don't get decisive, show commitment, discipline, and perseverance, this book will never become successful. The person you must always tell the truth to yourself. The promises you must always keep are the ones you make to yourself. As such, the best way to make sure you keep the promise you made when you signed that binding book writing contract is to give yourself weekly goals.

Have specific, measurable, aspirational, reasonable, and timed (S.M.A.R.T) goals that you must reach every week. An excellent way to go is setting yourself, weekly word counts. I gave you a rough word count of the various books you might write. Use that rough estimate as a reference to break down your writing goals. Of course, you might need to adjust once you have an outline of the book ready, so be flexible with the final estimated word count but become very serious about writing a specific amount of words each week. I started with weekly, but nowadays, I do daily word count goals, where I will set 2,000 words as my daily goal. You can set 3,500 words as your weekly limit, which means you only need to write 500 words per day.

And I also want you to commit to finishing the book and sending it out to your agent or self-publishing on a specific date.

Write this out:

I am so happy and grateful now that I [your name] have successfully [published/handed in the manuscript to my agent] on this day of [date].

Step Eleven: Focus on writing one chapter at a time and put blinders on everything else

As you start writing, I want you to take this one page and one chapter at a time. Sure, you have the whole vision of the book clearly outlined on your working area, but I urge you to shift your attention from dealing with the whole. Instead, focus on each piece that will eventually make the whole.

Most authors start getting overwhelmed when they sit to write because they are trying to deal with the entire book all at once. Save yourself the unnecessary pressure. It will also help motivate you and decrease the tendency to procrastinate when you know all you have to focus on is one chapter.

Step Twelve: Don't edit anything

It is a common one for perfectionists, but if you want to be a great writer, you've got to throw perfectionism out the window and allow yourself to be a kindergarten kid playing with arts and crafts.

Lousy work is excellent and accepted at this phase of your writing.

Step Thirteen: Write every day

For best results, once you start the work and set your weekly milestones, the best practice is to keep at it every single day until the draft is complete. If your business and family demands cannot accommodate daily writing, then consider customizing your unique schedule. One entrepreneur decided to write on the weekends. Each weekend he writes a chapter. At the end of six months, his book will be ready to publish as long as he remains consistent. You can do the same.

Step Fourteen: Don't look things up as you write

It is a huge mistake many of us make. I have been guilty of it at times, and what I realize is that it makes your writing slower and less enjoyable. If you have a quote or reference you want to insert within the book, try this instead. Insert a note for yourself where the quote needs to be. Going back to the example of my email-marketing book, I would do this: [Quote from Seth Godin about marketing goes here]. Then once I get to the second phase of my writing, I would fill in those blanks.

Step Fifteen: Don't use big words

Using jargon that only people in your industry know (or acronyms you made up) will only turn off your readers because they won't be able to follow. It's also not a great idea to write for the modern audience in the formal academic language with words that are not used in ordinary conversations since the 19th century. Unless, of course, you are writing for academics. But if you intend to become an Amazon bestseller, you better write as you speak because people today want laid back type of communication. Be clear, concise, and assume an eighth-grader will be reading the book.

Step Sixteen: Before editing the book, do this. Let the book marinate for at least a day

Then read it out loud to yourself. It isn't something you'll hear a lot of authors talk about, but it's truly an important step. Once the draft is ready to go to the next phases of editing and polishing, let it sit for at least a day (I recommend longer) and give yourself that break.

Focus on something that has nothing to do with your writing project. When you're ready, sit down with a cup of tea and go through the draft at various intervals. It will help you see areas you may have missed, sections that need to be changed or reframed, word flow, story flow, etc. Highlight all the areas that require adjustments.

That way, when it's time to edit and polish, you'll be viewing it with fresh eyes, and you'll know just what needs to be adjusted. Here are a few questions to help you transition from the first draft to the editing phase.

- Does my introduction grab the attention of my reader?
- How can I strengthen my arguments even more?
- Have I spotted any weakness in my chapters, and are there chapters that need to be chopped/rewritten?
- Is there flow from one chapter to the next?
- Is the central idea easily identifiable?

If you feel content with the new version and rewrites, it's time to move to the next step.

Step Seventeen: Editing

This phase requires time, and if you want the best results, it also requires some investment of resources. You can rewrite, edit, proofread, and polish the book all by yourself, or you can choose to hire a professional to help. It will accelerate the writing process itself and ensure you're creating a book readers will enjoy.

However, if you have no budget allocation for a professional, take your time, and simply go through the book, revise it as many times as will be necessary. You can also enlist the help of friends and family to help you with the editing.

Step Eighteen: Beta readers

The only thing worse than not finishing a book is writing a book that no one relates to. To avoid the heartbreak of writing something no one will ever read, get some feedback from a few people as early on as possible. As soon as the first draft is ready, I encourage you to select a few beta readers. It can be friends, family, or a fan club. Some authors even prefer to get feedback once they are only a few chapters in. I find that too distracting, but check in with yourself to see what resonates with you.

The critical thing to remember here is that you need to create a book that you enjoy writing, and one that your readers will enjoy devouring. Don't do it all on your own. Get that necessary feedback to make sure you're moving in the right direction.

Step Nineteen: Polishing the final touches

Writing and publishing your book are very different skills. The writing part of the book is what we've mostly covered in this book, but let's not forget the publishing part, which comes with its own set of requirements. However, before you can be ready to deal with publishing and marketing, you'll have to make sure the book is well polished, professional, and appealing to the audience.

I recommend making a plan beforehand and deciding how much professional help you are willing to invest in. If you can hire an editor, a proofreader, and a publishing agent, then most of your work will be done as soon as you go through the editing phase. The last details of the book which include formatting, artworks, proofreading, etc. can all be taken care of, but if you don't have any help, this is the part where you roll up your sleeves and prepare for a steep learning curve.

Try your best to seek help because often you are too close to the book to execute on these minor details (which matter a lot).

Step Twenty: Commit to releasing it

Commit to finishing the book no matter what, and regardless of how scary it feels, release it to the world even if it doesn't feel completely ready or perfect. In truth, the book is never really prepared if you ask the author. So don't just sit on it, release it on Amazon, send it to your publisher or do whatever needs to be done to get it in front of the right people. Withholding the book from the world once it's written will prevent you from growing, succeeding, and becoming a better author. Share your ideas with the world freely and trust that you did your best.

What to do if you get stuck or lose focus?

Before sending you off to implement on everything we've shared in this book, it's essential to give you some tools that you can use when the going gets tough. Although I do hope you don't end up getting writer's block or losing concentration, I am well aware of how common it is.

I have struggled with writer's block on many occasions, and I wish I could give you a single formulaic cure that cannot fail to work. Here's the thing. Writing is an art, a very subjective experience, whether one is writing fiction or nonfiction. So, becoming a better writer doesn't have a one size fits all solution. There is no magic antidote to heal you when the trials and tribulations of writing wound you. Even in writing my book, whenever I had to wrestle with an enemy standing in the way of my accomplishments, I had to test out different approaches. Each victory was very different, and it took experimentation to find something that worked for that particular situation.

Therefore, I want to make sure this book also provides as many practical tips as possible so that you can have enough tricks up your sleeve when the going gets tough.

Robyn Mallory was halfway through her first "How-to" book. She'd been wanting to self-publish and share her knowledge of bootstrapping a beauty brand for the last ten years. When she first started writing, she thought this project would be easy as pie that it would pale in comparison to the effort it took to go from zero to six figures in her business. In fact, during a couple's dinner with her best friend since high school, she said, "I think I can probably do this project in my sleep. I'm giving myself six weeks tops to get it published, and that's just because I also have a launch coming up, so I'm trying to be modest here about my superwoman powers." Boy, was she wrong!

At some point it got so bad, she would sit down for her allocated hour of writing in the morning, and get nowhere. Every five minutes, she would get up to do something. Either grab some water, check to see if the dog was okay, etc. She caught herself staring blankly outside the window a few times as well. Even when she tried to force herself to focus, she would soon develop the urge to grab another snack, check emails, and respond to the incoming text messages from her husband. At the end of the hour, there were only 50 words on the page!

"I tried to write this morning, and it was a nightmare. I was completely blank. That's three weeks in a row now. Trying to squeeze out the next word feels so horrible I want to throw in the towel."

And I know she's not the only one. Many writers tell stories of hair-pulling hours, days, or even months. Part of becoming a great writer is going through the writing journey, which always involves the inevitable dry spell where you feel as though there isn't a creative bone left in you. When the well seems to dry up, how you handle yourself at that moment is probably far more important than why the block happened. But I know how curious writers can be, so here are some common causes that experts blame for this horrid experience.

1. **Fear** - Many writers get to a point where they start being overly self-conscious and self-doubt creeps in.

    Be warned, that learned voice of judgment that always second-guesses you will pop up. It might make you criticize your work too much. You might start feeling inadequate or insecure about your writing capabilities. Fear is a primary culprit when it comes to failure and books that never get written. Don't fall for it.

2. **Perfectionism** - The common human tendency to want everything to be "just right" will harm rather than help you.

    It's excellent for Goldilocks to seek out things that are just right, but if you want to succeed, you'll have to leave this idea of perfection on the sidelines and jump in the deep end knowing that it's going to get messy, but in the end, it will all work out.

3. **Fatigue** - If you're not getting enough rest, it will be hard to keep up with daily demands and still create a fantastic book. Sleep directly affects your concentration levels, your creativity, productivity, and mood. Writing is a very creative, artistic (and in my case, spiritual) experience. Check inward often to see how energized and well-rested you are, especially if your creativity seems to be tanking.

4. **Stress** - This is a big one for entrepreneurs. We wear many hats, and every day feels like an ongoing Olympic marathon.
Although some medical research has found that not all stress is bad for you, too much of it will carry adverse effects. Stress from your family obligations, work-related stress, financial stress, the pressure to complete the book, and so on can become a hindrance to you doing your best work. If you are experiencing overwhelm and stress as you write a book, take a break for a while, and remedy that feeling first. Creativity flows more easily when one is at ease and in the flow.

5. **Timing** - Speaking about flow, do you know what happens when you try to force a book out of you? Nothing good. Remember that!
Sometimes, you might get an idea for a book, and you might feel there's something in you that needs sharing with the world, but it might

not feel like the right time. When I was writing my third book, I received the central idea just a few months after publishing my second book. But I could tell I needed it to sit and stew a little longer before writing it, and I gave myself the grace to remain in that "pregnancy" phase until I knew it was the right time. When I finally started working on it, getting into the flow of writing came more natural, and I was able to crank it out in just 90 days. It is something a lot of people don't know. There is a difference between procrastination (putting it on hold out of fear, confusion, or overwhelm) and timing. Learn to recognize within your pattern as you go through this project when an idea is going through incubation and requires time.

For Robyn, the best solution she found was getting a writing coach to help her through the rest of the book until completion.

I'm going to assume; you'd rather avoid that same pit of despair. If so, take the following tips and add them to your writing toolbox.

Switch off all distractions before sitting to write

Turn off notifications from your computer, close all unnecessary windows, put your phone on mute, shut the door, and turn off the TV or radio. Use a distraction-free word processor. Make sure you avoid and stop all distractions before switching to writing mode.

Silence external noise

For some people, external distractions kill their concentration. If this is you, I recommend using noise-canceling headphones. I use Bose, but you can also consider earplugs.

Hydrate more

The brain loses focus when you become dehydrated. Just because you're not doing any physical work doesn't mean you're not burning calories and exerting effort. Make sure you have a big bottle of water or lemon water next to you and hydrate frequently.

Freewrite

It is a must-do for all writers. It's a great way to generate new thoughts and ideas. Start by writing about anything you feel like writing. It shouldn't be about the book you're working on unless you want it to be. Once you have a prompt, set a short time for yourself and then just write anything and everything that comes into mind. I like to take superhero characters that I love and create little scenes for them for about twenty minutes. It refreshes my mind and soul a lot, plus it's entertaining.

Spend some time laughing or speaking with someone uplifting

At times, all you need is to break from your world and give your attention to someone else that makes you feel good. Consider calling up a friend or family member who makes you feel good and have lunch or coffee together. Spend time listening to them and talking about topics that excite you. The less you focus on your block, the faster it will phase off, and you never know, you might just evoke a new idea from listening to other people.

Get physical

By this, I mean get your ass off the chair and run, dance, do yoga, Pilates, weight lifting, or whatever else you enjoy. Moving your body gets your energy flowing. Writer's block is always going to occur when energy stagnates within us. The easiest way to get the energy flowing again in the brain and body is through physical exercise. I recommend adding some kind of exercise routine to your daily writing ritual. If you don't have a writing routine, it's time to get one.

The Pomodoro technique

It is a simple, customizable technique that you can employ to make sure you focus 100% and take frequent breaks, which is also super important. I like to write for 25 minutes (full concentration) and then break for 5 minutes. You can choose to write for 45 minutes then take a 15-minute break.

I wouldn't recommend going longer than 45-50 minutes because the brain slows down at that point for all of us. By taking calculated short breaks, you give your mind the chance to reset.

One more thing to note here is when you take that short break, let it be to catch some fresh air, hydrate, dance, or whatever else will help you completely relax and come back to your writing with a sharp mind.

Always finish with a hook and some notes for yourself

It is a simple hack I learned from my mentor, which helps me tremendously. As soon as you finish writing for that day, try to leave a few notes in your text to help you pick up where you left off the next time you sit to write. Leave yourself little teasers, a thought or idea you wish to expand on, etc. It helps especially when you're moving from one chapter to the next, and you only write over the weekends.

CONCLUSION

Setting unrealistic standards for yourself and expecting a unicorn ride with this project will not sustain you. It is a journey and a process that comes with its own set of obstacles and failures. Embrace the journey and permit yourself to fail forward. You can figure things out as you go, and you do have what it takes to write an impactful book. All you need is consistency and the steps laid out in the previous chapter.

But wait... What if for you the actual typing or writing is truly impossible?

Thanks to technology, I have a perfect solution for you too.

Recording and transcribing your book

Remember, at the start of this book; I promised to share a simple technique that would ensure you write a great book without ever typing a word? Well, here it is! And all you need is your little smartphone. That's right. You can speak your thoughts on the voice notes and compile them into short sections. Another cool hack is using Skype Recorder. It's free and easy to use. All you need is a friend who will be willing to listen to you as you speak and record on your topic. As you create each section, organize them into folders on your computer and send them out to be transcribed into a draft.

Once you have the written draft, you can choose to work on the editing or send it off to a professional ghostwriter to help you turn the words into a book. And thanks to platforms such as Rev.com, Upwork, and Fiverr, you can do it at a very affordable fee. So, you see, there isn't any reason your expertise, advice, experience, and story shouldn't be shared with the world. Now that you have all the necessary tools and know-how, it's time to roll up your sleeves and start working on your book. Whether you choose to write it by hand, type it on your keyboard, speak into your voice notes or voice record on Skype, creating your finished book is now a few steps away, and you have the exact blueprint that will successfully get you to the finish line.

The Journey to Overcoming Writer's Block

————— ✎✎✎✎ —————

Master Routines to Boost Your Creative Mind and Cure Procrastination Forever

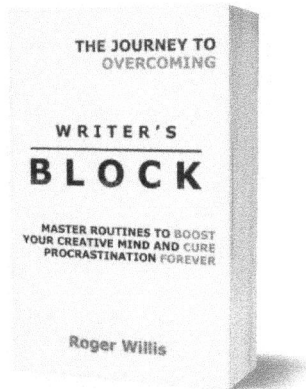

THE JOURNEY TO
OVERCOMING

WRITER'S
BLOCK

MASTER ROUTINES TO BOOST
YOUR CREATIVE MIND AND CURE
PROCRASTINATION FOREVER

Roger Willis

INTRODUCTION

> *"People on the outside think there's something magical about writing, that you go up in the attic at midnight and cast the bones and come down in the morning with a story, but it isn't like that. You sit in back of the typewriter and you work, and that's all there is to it."*
> *- Harlan Ellison*

You've been there, haven't you?

Staring at a blank notebook or empty document on your computer waiting for something to happen but nothing does. Four hours later, you're still in the same spot feeling drained and 250 words to show for it. What should you do? Succumb to the misery of feeling stuck and locked out of inspiration?

Creatives from all walks of life have experienced this block, not just writers. Inspiration can become so elusive as any creative person will tell you. Playwright, Paul Rudnick said:

> *"Writing is 90 percent procrastination: reading magazines, eating cereal out of the box, watching infomercials. It's a matter of doing everything you can to avoid writing, until it is about four in the morning and you reach the point where you have to write."*

Staying up until four in the morning may not be the case for every writer, but the man has a point. There's a lot of behind the scenes stuff that most writers don't divulge. For a novice just starting to work on their first or second book, things can get pretty scary when the process isn't as perfect as they'd pictured in their head. That's what this book is going to help you with — the imperfections and struggles of writing.

If you're one of those people who assume that a secret muse sits on the shoulders of great writers making sure they always have inspiration, then you're seriously naive.

Writing is hard work, takes discipline, and requires perseverance, consistency, and the right tools to turn into something substantial.

I dare you to find any good or great writer who does not testify to experiencing writer's block at some stage in their writing career. Even a prolific writer like Virginia Woolf struggled with feelings of inadequacy during her career. She said:

"Anyone moderately familiar with the rigors of composition will not need to be told the story in detail; how he wrote and it seemed good; read and it seemed vile; corrected and tore up; cut out; put in; was in ecstasy; in despair; had his good nights and bad mornings; snatched at ideas and lost them; saw his book plain before him and it vanished; acted people's parts as he ate; mouthed them as he walked; now cried; now laughed; vacillated between this style and that; now preferred the heroic and pompous; next the plain and simple; now the vales of Tempe; then the fields of Kent or Cornwall, and could not decide whether he was the most divine genius or the greatest fool in the world."

Indeed, every creative person has experienced that feeling of being dragged in the mud. It may not be a frequent occurrence, but I can assure you, it happens even to the best of us.

The main issue I have when I look around at books that inform on writer's block is that most people position the writer's block as the villain of your writing career. It is considered to be something horrible and negative. But what if that's not entirely accurate? What if the real culprit is your ignorance? Ouch! That's a tough one to swallow.

And if you are the type of writer looking for a book that will help validate and pin the blame on things that are beyond your control, then this isn't the book for you.

This book is for writers who genuinely want to increase their understanding of what writer's block is and how to best overcome it whenever it does show up. It is explicitly going to help you if you're the type of person that prefers to take ownership of your life and actions, rather than seek out excuses. And if that's you, then stick around, because I am about to give you some nuggets that will undoubtedly transform your perception of writer's block.

CHAPTER 1

What is Writer's Block?

"I suppose I do get 'blocked' sometimes but I don't like to call it that. That seems to give it more power than I want it to have. What I try to do is write. I may write for two weeks 'the cat sat on the mat, that is that, not a rat,' you know. And it might be just the most boring and awful stuff. But I try. When I'm writing, I write. And then it's as if the muse is convinced that I'm serious and says, 'Okay. Okay. I'll come.'"
- Maya Angelou

A two-time best-selling author recently shared with me that he has been stuck for four months on the story he's developing. He wrote a chapter, then felt the pull away from that piece to another. It was troubling for him because the first two books he's authored happened rather smoothly. And given the fact that he's a man who likes to keep his commitments and get work done, the delay with this upcoming book is starting to keep him up at night.

Raise your hand if you've been in a similar situation. My hand is definitely up! I could come up with numerous reasons why this author might be going through this "block" and will name most of them in just a bit, but before getting to that, I want to make you aware of the same truth I shared with him.

Writer's block is that state in which an author feels unable to proceed with his or her writing; when one cannot think of what to write next. Unfortunately, most people have turned it into some kind of a medical condition (which it isn't by the way), like a virus that takes control of the creative process and renders you inefficient. What's even crazier is that writers think that their case is special and unique, which, again - isn't.

Let me ask you this: Have you ever met a person working in a less creative career who complained about experiencing "blocks" the way we writers love to do? If you're honest, the answer is no. A cubicle dweller will complain about Monday Blues or the 3 p.m. slump but never about a creative block. In no other industry have I encountered professionals speaking about being prevented from doing their work by some unforeseen, all-powerful force that is beyond their control - except with creatives.

I'm not trying to be mean here, but I want to give it to you straight, so you can finally stop falling into the trap so many of us land in.

I think the reason we never hear about a "doctor's block" or an "engineer's block" is because few professions require the honesty and self-reflection that writing does. I mean, as a writer, we are continually mining our life experiences, and spinning that information into beautiful prose for the world to consume and enjoy. It is no joke, my friend, and from that vantage point, it's easy to see why writer's block does exist.

The block is your pre-emptive defense against judgment. It's an internal conflict, an invisible wall between yourself and the public, and usually the safety net answer that you give when you don't want to divulge any more information about the book you haven't written.

When you tell people you have writer's block, they offer empathy, compassion, and understanding. Best of all, they leave you alone without questioning the integrity of your work or your capabilities as a writer because of the blame for underperformance shifts to this invisible villain - writer's block.

So, if you genuinely want to overcome writer's block, you also need to get more real with yourself. Writer's block only exists in your head. It is not a medical condition or an external force more significant than you. It is something internal that can only be handled from within your creative mind.

What Causes Writer's Block?

Now that you've heard the harsh truth about what writer's block is, here's the real problem that's messing with your creative output.

- Fear
- Doubt
- Poor research
- Distractions
- Fatigue
- Imposter syndrome
- Lack of structure and organization
- Laziness
- Busyness
- Perfectionism

After writing daily for the last decade or so, I can assure you, fear and self-doubt remain the highest suspects whenever I hit a snag. I know every writer is different, so maybe your reality and the root cause behind your writer's block might be different. Still, in my fact, the biggest hindrance I encounter in my writing career, as well as those of fellow authors, boils down to fear.

Discovering what the root cause of your block is doesn't fix the problem. That's called gaining self-awareness, which is an essential first step. Once you do have awareness, action toward a resolution must take place. Writer's block will not magically fix itself. If you want to make writing a career and you want to get paid for what you write, it must become a habit.

So, here's a simple three-step process to help you go within and figure out what's holding you back.

STEP ONE:

Become aware and acknowledge the resistance

I want you to become aware of and recognize this growing within you that makes it hard to sit and write. Rather than seeing this block as something negative, I challenge you to see it as a tool that you can use to your advantage.

If you are experiencing resistance, it means there's a disconnect, and your creative juices will be restricted for whatever reason. It is your opportunity to level up as a writer and break new ground.

In life, we are either growing or dying. There is no such thing as neutral ground. And so even with your writing project, each new book is an experience that will cause you to grow and level up, especially when you do it right. You will never be the same person you were before starting this book.

So, when you realize consciously and subconsciously that your current "comfort zone" is being challenged, you should get all the more encouraged because the only time an internal conflict occurs, and our minds start to self-sabotage, is when something new and vital is well underway.

STEP TWO:

Name it to tame it

Now that you acknowledge there's nothing wrong with you and that your inner conflict is part of your growth, ask yourself what is going on? Why do you feel stuck or disconnected from your creative flow? It is the step where you identify the root problem - not the symptom.

Is it fear of failure? Is it fear of being rejected? Are you still battling with the feeling that you're not good enough? Do you feel like you're not talented enough, worthy enough, resilient enough? Or are you simply exhausted? What is it that underlies the symptoms you're experiencing?

For most of us, fear is the underlying root problem that causes a disconnect, and we end up feeling stuck.

One of my author friends worked for eighteen months to produce an epic romance novel, which ended up being a New York Times bestseller.

A few months after that success, he decided to work on a new book project. A few weeks into it, excitement turned into anxiety and worry because he felt the pressure of producing something as epic as the first book.

He was already stressing about getting the book published in time; he struggled with lots of insecurities, wondering if his best work was already behind him. He got scared about what his new raving audience would think of him if they saw how hard it was to complete the second chapter and worse yet, what if they thought it was a complete horse poop?

All these strangling thoughts while working on the book led to a severe block of his creativity. It was as though the characters from his book had taken a vacation, and he couldn't find them anywhere.

He tried walking, summoning them through meditation, drinking water, and lemon, but nothing happened. They had vanished! To the rest of the world, however, he was playing it cool, pretending that he didn't have "enough time" to work on the new book.

I only got to hear about the self-manufactured torture chamber he was living on one Friday night when he had a bit too much to drink and cracked under the influence. Until he was willing to release that tension, acknowledge that something was wrong, and indeed identify the underlying fears that block would hijack and hinder his progress.

STEP THREE:

Face your worst fears

The next step for you is to summon your courage, get your game face on, and play out your worst-case scenario. In other words, go face to face with that lion that's on your path. Usually, when I do this, I discover the lion was a stuffed teddy. So, at this point, having determined what's wrong, ask yourself - what's the worst that could happen if I did fail? Would that destroy my entire career? Would I die? Most of the time, our worst fears only seem life-threatening and paralyzing because they are hiding behind the shadows of mental darkness. Bring those thoughts and fears out into the light, scrutinize them objectively, and you realize that fear doesn't hold much water.

I used to struggle with the fear of failure. Writing something that no one appreciates or enjoys. And so, I decided whenever that thought or emotion came up during my writing, I would schedule a face-to-face meeting and play out the worst-case scenario. Could I fail with this book? Sure. Would that destroy my entire career in one stroke? Not likely. I would need lots of failures before I would be entirely out of the game. Of course, it is possible to keep failing until my career flops, but it's certainly not likely. Think of Michael Jordan. He is one of the greatest basketball players in history. Yet even he's a pro at failure. In the Nike commercial that Jordan did, he explained that he missed more than 9000 shots in his career. He has lost almost 300 games; failed 26 times when he was trusted to take the game-winning shot, and yet, he is still one of the greatest players. How about instead of getting tormented by what could go wrong, we focus on how amazing it will be when things go right.

> *"The best way is to always stop when you are going good and when you know what will happen next. If you do that every day, you will never be stuck. Always stop while you are going good and don't think about it or worry about it until you start to write the next day. That way your subconscious will work on it all the time. But if you think about it consciously or worry about it, you will kill it and your brain will be tired before you start."*
> *- Ernest Hemingway*

CHAPTER 2

Where Does Inspiration Come From?

"Creativity is an energy. It's a precious energy, and its something to be protected. A lot of people take for granted that they're a creative person, but I know from experience, feeling it in myself, it is a magic; it is an energy. And it can't be taken for granted."
- Ava DuVernay

Inspiration is a tough one to grasp logically, unlike motivation. If you look all around the Internet, what you would find is a lot of motivation. Coaches, speakers, and so-called gurus are all great at motivating the masses with videos, quotes, etc. Goal Cast is a brand that is made entirely of motivational content extracted from interviews and speeches of famous people, and they have amassed an enormous following. People love to be motivated, and many have become addicted to receiving it daily, like a drug or an espresso shot to boost adrenaline. Inspiration, on the other hand, is a different story. And it's the very thing every true writer needs to do in his or her best work. But where does it come from? Is it finite? Can you run out of it?

There was a time in my life where I believed the commonly preached B.S. that inspiration depends on one's talent. That it's finite, like a vein of quartz within a lump of rock and once mined it dries up.

The truth is, we all have unlimited potential, and there is no end to what you can do or become regardless of age, experience, or skills. Inspiration springs up from within you in continuous flow unless you create barricades or clog out those pipes that connect you to the boundless storehouse of life itself. My conviction today is that you can relate to inspiration. It's a stream, which you can discover, and as a channel for this inspiration, you can allow your work, ideas, and creativity to flow through you to show incredible results.

Inspiration comes from within you and gets activated and nurtured by your state of mind; all the things you absorb in your environment, and re-assimilate can turn into something unique and beautiful. That's why many writers speak of spending time visiting art galleries, museums, or being in nature doing activities that are entirely unrelated to writing. It's about finding experiences that make you feel more like you (the best version of yourself) and tapping more into that so that once you step back into your work, you can bring forth the message you genuinely wish to share with the world.

Mark-Anthony Turnage, a composer, once said, "forget the idea that inspiration will come to you like a flash of lightning. It's much more about hard graft."

It's easy to feel inspired to write when you're in the zone; when your muse is right there in front of you, and all conditions are just right. But I want to focus on those times when you have to write, but nothing comes to mind. Thinking about the fact that you feel stuck only elevates the problem, and since frustration is painful, you procrastinate even more. Time ticks by; you feel the deadline creep closer, and the inspiration continues to slip away as your anxiety grows. What can you do during those times?

Stop forcing yourself to feel inspired, stop being passive about it, and stop waiting for it to fall on your lap while lying on your couch because it won't. I know you've heard from many artists this notion that inspiration can just strike out of nowhere. One moment you're in complete darkness; the next, you're off to the races. The Greeks came up with the concept of a "Muse" for this very reason. But waiting on a flash of creative energy seemingly from the gods of creativity isn't always the best idea, especially if you're serious about overcoming a block.

There are simple things you can do that can help stir up your inspiration and connect you back to that high-flying streak of creativity. After starting famous writers and other artists, I have compiled together a few hacks of my own to help produce my flow of inspiration whether or not my Muse is playing hard to get.

Nurture and nourish yourself with activities and experiences that fill you up as a person.

You must remember that you cannot pour water from an empty vessel. Half the battle of overcoming your block is about figuring out how to refill and refuel yourself.

Learn something completely new.

For me, this helps stir up my creativity and inspiration, especially when I learn something that's totally off my comfort zone.

It could be an online course on marketing, coding, or drawing. These seemingly unrelated activities to your current project (as long as you enjoy it) could all help inspire some new type of creativity. Sometimes, you don't even have to finish the course.

Learn to mute out that voice that speaks negatively about your work.

It is something we must all learn to do because learning to silence that voice of internal judgment has a direct impact on our creativity and inspiration.

There's nothing wrong with being critical of your work, maybe even comparing your past work with the present or with peers that you admire, but when it comes to actual writing, you need to be all invested. You must believe that you've got what it takes.

Ask yourself questions you can't answer.

I find that going above and beyond ordinary human awareness and logic helps me reconnect with that frequency of creativity that I like.

Who am I? Why am I here? What is the meaning of life? Does any of this really matter? What is eternity? These are all questions that none of us have definite answers to but could help stir up something within you that jumpstarts your creative flow.

Knowing that you have access to an endless stream of inspiration and creativity is one thing. Being able to keep that connection unimpeded is another. Often even when we do make this realization, we still get caught up in belief systems that create blocks. Your beliefs play a significant role in the creation of your conditions, so find a way to work on getting the right perspective. Creativity and inspiration are yours anytime you need it as long as you don't let the causes described in chapter two get in the way.

"If you get stuck, get away from your desk. Take a walk, take a bath, go to sleep, make a pie, draw, listen to music, meditate, exercise; whatever you do, don't just stick there scowling at the problem. But don't make telephone calls or go to a party; if you do, other people's words will pour in where your lost words should be. Open a gap for them, create a space. Be patient."
- Hilary Mantel

CHAPTER 3

What's Holding You Back?

If you've read each word and made it this far, there are a few assumptions I can make about you. You want to become a great writer with stunning works of art that readers can't stop talking about. Maybe this has been a dream of yours since childhood, and you want to produce books that touch hearts and change lives. It could be a full-time career or something part-time but one thing for sure, you've read every piece of advice you could find. Write every day! Sit on the keyboard and bleed. Create daily rituals, and don't skip them at all costs. Forget all that! I mean, if it were working, you wouldn't be reading a book on overcoming writer's block. You need a different approach because something's still holding you back from unleashing your full potential.

What I want to do (with your permission) is to redirect your efforts into something more unconventional. As I said before, your writer's block exists within you. So, the thing that's holding you back isn't going to be solved by any

95

external force. More often than not, what holds you back comes from a developed habit, not a one-time thing. We are creatures of habit, and these habits either support us as we move toward our goals or hinder us from undermining our ability to achieve. I won't sugarcoat this. Becoming a great writer is going to be difficult, especially if you're living with a slew of habits that aren't supportive of your goals. Do a self-check now to see if any of these pokes something within you.

You get sidetracked easily

For example, it's time to write, but before you start, this urge to answer just one quick email or quickly scroll through Facebook suddenly takes over. Pretty soon, your allocated writing time is over, and you've barely written a page of your book. So, you promise yourself you'll do better next time, but we all know what that develops into overtime.

You feel the need to be perfect

Continually striving for perfection sets you up for failure as a writer. Stephen King, a prolific writer who has sold hundreds of millions of books, many of which are made into movies and comics, shares solid advice, *"Write with the door closed, rewrite with the door open."* Writing is intimate, and you should feel free enough to be raw and real with your words, especially at first. Have you been setting unattainable standards for yourself?

Old wounds and past failures weigh you down.

Just because something didn't work out in the past doesn't mean it won't work out now. Failure is part of becoming successful. I have learned to wear my failures and rejections like badges of honor, and you be should too. No one ever succeeds without experiencing some kind of failure.

"Carrie" by Stephen King was rejected 30 times before finally being accepted by a publisher. "Harry Potter and the Sorcerer's Stone" was rejected 12 times, and J.K. Rowling was told, *"not to quit her day job!"* This list is endless, not just with writers but even artists. For example, Jay-Z had to start his record label to publish his music because no one else believed in him (and he's now a billionaire by the way). All this to say, failure and rejection should not be the poison that destroys your potential for greatness.

You're always looking for approval

Seeking and waiting for approval or validation can also hold you back and create a block in your creativity. If you get too caught up in what others think of you (including your audience), then you'll stop actively listening within where real insights and inspiration come from. Training to gain the approval of others is futile and could easily hold you back. It isn't to say you shouldn't take in feedback and opinion from others. There is a time and a place for that. You are your own person, living with your reservoir of insights, and a message of truth that you are to channel through this book. To make it work, you really must learn to stand on your own two feet. There is no other way to become a great writer.

You have self-doubt

It is by far the biggest issue I feel most writers face. It is a dream killer and the poison that disconnects you from your creativity and inspiration. Self-doubt is such a big issue I am discussing it more in-depth in the next chapter. The critical thing to realize here is that as long as self-doubt dials up, every attempt to produce something incredible will be stymied up.

You underestimate the importance of discipline and persistence

A lot of writers start hot and motivated then quickly fizzle out because they fall for the flawed assumption that talent and lots of caffeine are all you need to write a book. Sure, skill helps, and if you are that type of writer who needs caffeine, you'll want to stock up. But what it comes down to is discipline and persistence. That is what gets you to the finish line. You've got to figure out a way to stick to your project, work tirelessly and enthusiastically until you see it through. I'm sharing more about this in the last chapter of this book.

CHAPTER 4

How to Deal with Self-Doubt

A study was conducted not too long ago about genius. The exploration was around trying to understand what happens in a person's life that is living what might be called a genius life. The research began with the premise that "genius" is the number of modalities with which one takes in information and can synthesize or make use of that information. What the researchers discovered was that the number of patterns (you know you could receive information in with your five senses and also intuitively, imaginatively, intellectually, and perceptively) were all common to every one of us. We all possess the ability to take in information through all these different mediums. However, when all are working together in harmony, like an entire orchestra, there is what we call genius.

So, they were exploring what happens in people's lives who live this genius life, and they discovered that almost ninety-nine percent of all

101

babies operate at a genius level for roughly the first eighteen to twenty-four months of their lives.

And if you pause to think this through for a moment, it does make sense. I mean the learning curve each one of us goes through to be able to discover how to control our hands and legs is incredible. If you watch a little infant staring at their hand or foot, it's as if it is something apart from themselves. The baby must learn how to incorporate bringing the whole body into a system, and they must shape ideas, learn words, crawl, and eventually walk. All this learning occurs in that first phase of life, and it's hyper-accelerated. In my opinion, those first few months of life have such a huge learning curve, perhaps beyond anything most of us ever achieve for the rest of our lives. Think about it: We do come into this world as geniuses.

According to the study, by the time we are five years old, only twenty percent of us are operating at a genius level. By the time we are twenty, only two percent are working at a genius level! What the heck happens to us? What mutes out those capacities that are ours?

Well, the research said that the disconnect occurs systematically and over long periods. And all of it can be attributed to this one thing: The learned voice of internal judgment.

We start to doubt. We make ourselves wrong and get into the habit of looking outside ourselves for strength, validation, approval, and opinions about what we can be, what we can do, and what's possible for us.

In other words, that research helped me realize that as we grow up, we learn to be condition-based in our thinking because that is the primary programming on planet earth. That's how most people live their entire lives. And perhaps that's fine if you spend your entire career in a cubicle, but for us as writers, it becomes a significant hindrance to our success.

The root cause of self-doubt is fear itself, and there are many variations of it, but the bottom line is you will struggle and continue to battle with failure and writer's block if you don't get a handle on that voice that generates self-doubt.

Your self-doubt is to you as kryptonite is to Superman. It's also the culprit behind imposter syndrome. It is one emotion we all struggle with, and it can ruin everything because the more we question ourselves and second guess our actions, the more our creativity gets stifled. Think of it this way: the biggest clogger creating a block in your flow of creativity and inspiration is almost always fear and self-doubt.

Jenny, an award-winning writer, shared her frustrations with me a few weeks ago:

"I'm not clinically depressed per se, but I have times when the self-doubt is so rampant, I have a hard time focusing on my work. I worry a lot. I'm anxious about

103

how I'll make a living as a writer. I love it, but so far, it's only made me enough money for a nice dinner. I'm also worried people won't like the book I'm currently working on because I'm not sure the themes are deep enough. And I keep wondering if the characters are well developed. It's crippling. And I'm so afraid to fail, which is odd considering I don't have much to fail from. I try to remind myself that things will work out, but it's easier said than done, you know?"

I think we can all agree that we've experienced similar frustrations. Self-doubt is creativity poison that creeps up on new writers as well as full-time professionals. Making money, getting famous, or becoming successful doesn't eliminate self-doubt, but the right kind of strategies can help you deal with it for good. Here are a few good ones to test out.

Strategies for Handling Self-Doubt:

Look at the story itself

Just take a moment and ask yourself the following questions:

Why am I finding it difficult to trust my thoughts?
Why is the book failing to develop the way I want
it to?
Is it because I'm trying to fix it into the wrong
shape?
Have I lost sight of my Why?
Or is it something else?

Understand that having that negativity surging up
within isn't by accident. Self-doubt and fear take
up residence in your mental space for a good
reason, and as long as you take the time to assess
why you feel the way you do or why things are
going badly, you can quickly evict them and get
back to work.

Say stop

As soon as you become aware of the inner conflict
rising, don't let things spin out of control. Instead,
take yourself to an environment that energizes
you and have a talk with that doubtful part of
yourself. I usually go to the beach, a river, a lake,
a pond, or any other body of water I can easily find
and have a heart to heart with myself.

You could present the current situation to
yourself and say something like, "No! I say no. We
are not going down that road again." By doing
this, you are disrupting that thought pattern and
showing yourself who's boss in your mind.

Order a giant dose of optimism

Is there someone in your life who is always overflowing with enthusiasm, optimism, motivation, and that bubbly energy that makes everything more radiant? Call them up and arrange an in-person meeting. Spend some time with that person and let that optimism flow over to you.

Find your source of optimism

In the unlikely event that there is no one in your life to fill that order, consider finding a podcast, audiobook, YouTube channel, or a book that can help you shift your self-doubt into optimism. Any piece of material that can help you think constructively of this challenge should do the trick.

Some people swear by Tony Robbins and his loud, aggressive nature. For some, it's spiritual teachers or motivational speakers like Les Brown. Whatever works for you, just do it for a few sessions and let the doubts melt away.

Make a list of all your achievements

Bring to mind all the successful experiences you've had, even if they have nothing to do with writing. Recalling those moments of fulfillment and satisfaction is a great way to shift from fear and self-doubt because you show yourself how amazing you've been in the past.

Scientists tell us that our brains are conditioned to actively recall a negative experience, even though it's not healthy for us for survival reasons. I think when we were still living in caves next to wild animals, that was a good thing, but in today's world, you don't need a constant reminder of the mishaps.

What you need is a reminder of all the good you've been able to produce. Be real about this, and don't try to force yourself into something you don't believe.

If you revisit your past experiences and see how well things have gone many times despite those self-doubts, then it becomes easier to let go and refocus your energy and take positive actions going forward.

Stop beating yourself up about having self-doubt!

Doing this makes things only worse and more difficult, have you noticed? It becomes a vicious cycle and feels like you can't get out of a recurring time loop. Beating yourself up because you're not moving forward only keeps you stuck in the very state you're trying to escape.

What I like to do in these moments is to parent myself and soothe myself, as a mother would her young child. I show myself compassion and use kind, loving words with a very empathic tone whenever I speak to myself. Then instead of trying to solve the whole problem or get clarity over the entire book, I simply ask myself what's one tiny baby step I could take that day to feel like I had accomplished something. I find that shifting my focus to taking baby steps is a great way to rebuild my momentum with no pressure or grand expectations.

Use the magic statement

"You might be right, but..."

I use this statement all the time whenever that negative inner chatter comes up. For example, when the thought comes up, "people won't like this new book."

I immediately counter that thought with, " You might be right, but I won't know until I finish writing it and give them a chance to read it."

Or I might hear, "You're not a writer; people will discover that you're not that good soon."

My response to that is, " You might be right, but until that day comes, I will just keep playing this role because it feels nice thinking of myself as a writer."

See how easy it can be to catch those shots of poison and dissolve them? The earlier you seize them, the less damage they do. So, what responses can you create now using this magic statement?

CHAPTER 5

Tips on How to Manage Your Energy

Just as professional athletes prepare and train before participating in a competition, you should also get into the habit of prepping and training your mind to write before starting a new project. Writing takes up a lot of energy. Even though it may not seem like it, writing is every bit as demanding as physical labor, which means you're expending a lot of energy. Unless you find a way to keep generating that energy, it doesn't matter how much time you've got to complete a book. Each time you sit in front of your blank page, if your brain isn't cooperating, nothing good will happen. To help you avoid or at least get out of that uncomfortable situation, let's discuss good practices for writing:

1. You need to have a unique system. I call this the secret sauce for finishing your book. We delve into this in the last chapter of this book.

2. You must start taking care of your physical health. Unhealthy writers won't do as well or enjoy the process of writing (which is equally as crucial as finishing). Your mind and body are connected in ways that even science cannot fully comprehend. When the physical body is not thriving, the brain cannot thrive or perform well. The type or length of physical activity that you do doesn't matter; you just need to be fully immersed in it. And with physical activity comes watching how you fuel your body. I know it can be hard for you to stop working on a project to make a healthy meal. Grabbing a coffee and eating cereals for dinner is the more comfortable option, but if you want to succeed long-term as a writer and in life, invest in healthier eating habits.

3. You must train your brain. Have you read the book "Super Brain" by Dr. Deepak Chopra and Dr. Rudolph E. Tanzi? It's an epic revelation of how wrong we are about the brain and its potential. In the book, Dr. Chopra says, "One of the unique things about the human brain is that it can only do what it thinks it can do. The minute you say, "my memory isn't what it used to be..." you are training your brain to live up to your diminished expectations. Low expectations mean low results. The first rule of the super brain is that your brain is always eavesdropping on your thoughts. As it listens,

it learns. If you teach it about limitation, your brain will become limited."

Now imagine what you are training your brain into whenever you say, "I have writer's block." One of the best ways to start preparing your brain is to develop consistency with your schedule so that you can write at the same time each day. You should also check out the long list of strategies I've shared in the next chapter, as some of them are specifically designed to help with this.

4. You must intentionally design and maximize your focus and relaxation times. Yes, you read it right. It's not just about prioritizing your productivity and focus. You need relaxation just as much, so you need to find activities or experiences that help create that balance between output and input of your creativity and inspiration. Your mind and brain need time to reset. For some people, relaxation means doing absolutely nothing! That's not resting for me; it's torture!

Besides sleeping, I give my brain time to reset by doing things I consider fun like walking, shopping, listening to Opera, watching stand-up comedy, and sometimes playing chess. I have a friend who resets by spending some time in church a few days a week volunteering as well as going to the art museum. We are all unique as individuals, so find experiences that help inspire and invigorate you, then schedule them into your calendar.

5. Work on your discipline. Without discipline, you won't get very far. Most people don't realize that talent alone isn't enough to make anyone successful regardless of their chosen field. I love writing with all my heart; if I stopped writing, my whole world would crumble - and yet, even I have to apply a lot of discipline to perform at the level that I do. Discipline and perseverance are not negatives in the world of writing; they are pre-requisites as much as passion is. Let's talk more about how you can amp up your discipline.

Good Practices for Increasing Self-Discipline

- Start writing every day
- Get an accountability partner
- Consider starting a blog for your book
- Read every day
- Change your perception of willpower
- Set smaller S.M.A.R.T goals within your writing project
- Create a reward system for yourself
- Learn to embrace discomfort
- Cultivate physical, mental, and emotional self-care rituals
- Create habits that support your writing

- Leverage technology
- Shift your perception of hard work
- Redefine what success means to you
- Work on gaining control over your emotions
- Identify your weaknesses and build support structures around them
- Track and measure your progress

Increasing Your Productivity

If you take care of your mind, your mind will take care of you. It's as simple as that. There is no conspiracy trying to take down your writing empire unless you help fuel it from within.

There's no shortcut to maintaining focus and productivity. It will not come by default, especially as you get older. An exhausted, unhealthy, stressed out, and a negative mindset can only produce writings that are subpar at best. The more you feed and nurture your mind with the right stuff, the better it will serve you.

That means you need to be deliberate and intentional with your activities so that everything you do optimizes for success. If you want to write well, stay focused, inflow, and highly productive, you'll need to make some changes.

Last year I invested quite a significant amount of time researching productivity and came across Edward Deci, a researcher who wrote a book titled 'Why We Do What We Do.' In the book, Deci

113

explains that when someone has six positive interactions with one negative, they are 31% more productive. During his research, Deci noticed a trend in positive interactions vs. negative and how they each influence productivity. Fascinating stuff.

Simple as it seemed to me at the time, I decided to put this theory to the test. I started writing out on my journal each morning before getting into my writing - why I was grateful to be working on this particular book. At first, it was simple things like I'm thankful for my ability to write clearly and effectively communicate my message with the world. A few days in, even those simple sentences started disappearing because I felt like I had already named everything I appreciate about my work. But I refused to let myself off the hook, and one year later, I am still doing this exercise every day. I bring gratitude to each project I want to work on, and I shifted my perspective from "I have to do it" to " I want to do it."

Ready to become a brilliant writer? Here's what you need to do:

Establish habits that help you perform at an optimum level

For example, don't stay up till 3 am to write just because you've heard writers say it works. Maybe you are more of a morning person; staying up late would only lead to - you guessed it - writer's block.

Get to know your body clock

Following up on that first tip, you need to self-investigate and identify your most productive hours. We all have natural rhythms that influence our ability to focus and produce. The secret here is to match your writing time to your most productive hours of the day. Do you know your body clock?

Take regular mental breaks

Even a short break, when done strategically, can give you that burst of inspiration and creativity needed to get you to the next chapter. The moment you feel mental fatigue kicking in, step away from the screen even if it's just for a few moments. Go for a walk, stretch, or spend a few minutes outside soaking in some sun.

Declutter your workspace or desktop

I didn't just make this one up by the way, even though it resonates with me. Researchers have found that when there's too much stuff in your field of view, it has a measurable impact on productivity. They found that too much clutter causes people to lose brain power and necessary focus. I found that by cleaning up my desktop, my mind would feel calmer, open, and at ease, which somehow enables me to refocus and get back into it.

Start your gratitude journal

Your creative mind can be immensely boosted by adopting a habit of gratitude for your writing. Developing appreciation for the story you're attempting to share with the world will increase your love of writing. Keep things simple. Write what you are grateful for, and why, every day for the next 30 days, and take note of the difference it makes. Here are a few starter lines to get you going.

I am grateful for my first cup of coffee this morning because it's exactly what I need to jump into my writing fired up.

I am grateful for my computer and writing software because they make my work super easy and convenient, and my writing software keeps all online distractions away from me.

Now it's your turn.

CHAPTER 6

Strategies for Overcoming Writer's Block

Reconnect with your WHY

Simon Sinek is famous for stating - always begin with your WHY. I think this is sound advice to apply whenever you bump into that writer's block. If the words just aren't streaming through, no matter what you try, step away from that situation and take a moment in solitude.

Sit with yourself in silence and remind yourself why you are working on this project. Why is it so vital that you put this book out in the world? What is this message you want to share, and why does it matter? Get reacquainted with your reason for writing and watch that block dissolve.

Stop obsessing over that, which is beyond your control

Instead of worrying over things that you can't control, such as what the public and critics will say, whether it'll become a bestseller in record time or not, etc., focus on the next thing you're going to write. Not the entire manuscript; just that next part.

Stop writing for the world

Getting published, building a fan base, becoming famous, and making money are all great, but none of them should be the driving motive behind your writing. The point of writing is the joy of sitting down to a blank page and crafting something beautiful or funny or heart wrenching or even just meh (depending on the day). Writing is more about the journey than the destination.

All this to say, writing is a form of self-expression, not an ego boost. Get back to writing for the joy it brings you, and that sense of "stuckness" will dissipate naturally.

Give yourself time

Sometimes I think all this pressure we put on ourselves as writers chokes our creativity like weeds on a rose bush. Sometimes it's best to step back, take some time self-reflecting, reading, discovering new things, learning about being a better writer, etc. When you feel like you're facing an invisible wall, don't force things and certainly don't try to hurry things along or fuss about deadlines. There's no rush to get published, and you are allowed to take your time. Always remember that.

Stop making excuses

Yes, this is imperative because, as I said at the beginning of this book, writer's block is real only in your head. So, this idea that you can justify your procrastination and avoidance with this term, just because everyone makes it seem acceptable is total B.S. If you are experiencing that inner conflict that blocks you from your zone of genius, do something about it. Realize it's there and acknowledge that it is your responsibility to overcome this temporary setback, from this figure out the best course of action that most resonates with you.

Challenge yourself

By this, I mean, you should seek to find something constructive in this experience. It's not all bad. There are lessons to be learned, insights to be gained, and growth to be experienced that can better assist your progress as a writer. This dry gap and discomfort can be a time for you to challenge your writing skills even more. See this block as a tool and stepping stone to help elevate you to the next level. Start by listing down all the good that can come from going through this experience.

Freewrite

Set a timer and give yourself that time to freewrite. If no words come to you, then use that time jotting down loose associations and images that come to mind relative to your story. Practice what's known as stream of consciousness writing. The only rule with this tip is that your pen has to keep moving for the entire time. Not all ideas will be of value, but you might find something that can then pull you back into the actual story you want to tell.

Permit yourself to suck

That's right. I want you to allow yourself to do some bad writing. In the book "Bird by Bird" by Anne Lamott, readers are encouraged to write terrible first drafts. Lammot reassured us that we all write bad first drafts and that the lousy first draft is part of the natural progression on the path toward an excellent second draft and a great manuscript. Set aside this illusion that you need to be great right off the bat. When you were learning to walk as a child, you didn't focus on being perfect; you concentrate on making it happen. That same childlike approach should be used in your creative endeavors. By taking on that carefree approach, you'll find the pressure is gone, and I'm pretty sure even your initial work won't be half as bad as you think. Besides, if it is terrible, no one else has to see it until you're ready.

Take regular breaks

Taking breaks regularly to reset your brain, refuel and hydrate your body must be prioritized. I noticed that when I don't stop at my appointed breaks, I end up being less productive on that given day. I like to use the Pomodoro technique to make sure my breaks are planned out well.

The Pomodoro Technique

This time management technique is used widely by people across diverse industries and works like a charm for me. Invented by Francesco Cirillo in the late 1980s, it's the perfect way to break your writing into intervals, avoid fatigue, and promote productivity. Here's how to implement it. Set the mini-goal you'd like to accomplish for the day. Set the Pomodoro for twenty-five minutes and work uninterrupted on that single writing task until the timer goes off. When the Pomodoro rings, pause, take your short break. You can grab a fresh cup of coffee, soak in some sun by the window, balcony, or go outside for a few minutes, or you can do anything else that is not work-related. I like to take my mandala and color them during my short breaks while doing deep breathing exercises. After the short break, jump back into it for another session.

After four Pomodoros, take a more extended break for about 20 or 30 minutes. The way I plan out my writing time, this long break is usually for healthy eating, light exercise, or being outdoors.

There are many ways to customize and make your Pomodoro more effective, depending on your objectives and preferences. Some writers set their Pomodoro to forty-five minutes. I don't recommend anything longer because studies have shown the brain tends to tune out anyways after that duration.

Handwrite your stream of consciousness

Even if you're stuck on the current manuscript, you can still write something. We've all heard the famous statement, "a body in motion tends to remain in motion..." Make sure you write something, anything at all. It could be an entirely new story, your current feelings, an experience you just had, or whatever else comes to you. There is no right or wrong - just write.

Change locations

If you usually write in silence in the corner of the room in your basement, switch things up and spend a day in a coffee shop or a library.

Sometimes the radical shift in the environment is enough to jumpstart your creative ideas.

Read a lot more than usual

You're already feeling stuck. Rather than forcing yourself to do something you're not aligned with at this moment, use this time to immerse yourself in a great book. Other people's writing can become an endless source of ideas, and who knows, something in there might get you back in the mood and inspire new thoughts.

Play

I'm being serious here. Pick a game you love that gets you all excited and immerse yourself in that for a few hours. I usually go to chess or LEGOS.

Shift your focus to someone who makes you feel good

How about interviewing a friend or just buying them coffee and spending some time with them so you can completely forget about work. Talk, laugh, listen, ask questions, and, most importantly, do something nice for them and notice the difference this makes in how you feel about yourself and life in general. Often, we like to think that work is separate from the home, but in truth, all things have a connection. The more you feel good about yourself, the more everything you do will reflect that.

Increase your physical activities

There's no better time to move your body, get a little sweat on, and improve your health than when your writing hits a snag. Perhaps your mind is trying to create some spare time for you to take care of your body. And research proves that working out improves all areas of your life, including creativity. So rather than sitting there watching Netflix or wallowing in self-pity, waiting for the writing gods to have mercy on you, go for a jog in the park or take a spin class.

Advanced strategies for overcoming writer's block

Get more structured

If you're one of those writers who scoff at the structure as something that would limit your creativity or even amplify writer's block, I'm sorry to say that's fear talking.

I am part of a writer's community where we meet up in person every three months to support, encourage, and keep each other accountable. There's a woman who joined our community about eighteen months ago, and each time she speaks, her main issue is always getting stuck halfway into her projects. During our last meet-up, I asked her what she's doing to resolve this recurring problem permanently. I brought in the concept of creating structure, and she immediately shrieked. "I'm not the type. I hate structure in my life and certainly can't write if I was forced to be more structured and organized."

Unfortunately, that mindset will keep you falling into the pit of writer's block. You need to find a way to make productivity not just probable, but inevitable.

Sleep on it

Sometimes the best medicine is to rest more. There are times when exhaustion, fatigue, or poor sleeping habits impact our ability to concentrate and focus. I found a research paper that speaks to this very truth. You can find a link to read the comprehensive research on how sleep works and the creative brain during sleep in the resource section at the end of the book. But here are some interesting insights on REM sleep and creativity.

Many people report being able to do their best work immediately after awakening. What is so special about the early morning? Research suggests the proximity to recent sleep is the key, especially given that most people have their longest stage of REM sleep just before waking in the morning. A Harvard Medical school study scientist reported that subjects could solve 30% more anagram word puzzles when tested after waking up from REM sleep than non-REM sleep. Most research published in 2012 similarly found that sleep is particularly good at helping people solve complex problems. Science has also confirmed that REM sleep allows people to become more creative. At the University of California at San Diego, researchers used a protocol called a Remote Associates Test (RAT) to quantify increases in creativity. They divided test subjects into three groups right before taking the test. One group was allowed to rest but not sleep, another was allowed to experience NREM sleep but was roused before REM, and the other was allowed to reach the REM stage. Those in the rest and NREM groups showed no increase in creativity as measured by RAT, whereas those recently woken from REM showed an increase in capacity. UC San Diego scientists also found that participants scored 40% better on a creativity test after REM sleep. REM seems to spark solutions to new creative problems better than any other stage of sleep, suggesting that "sleep on it" may be sound advice.

Need I say more?

Mind map your ideas

It is especially useful when you start feeling unclear about the direction of the story or if you're struggling with the progression of the story. A mind map is a diagram used to organize information visually. This term was coined by a British author and Television personality Tony Buzzan and can be an effective way to get you out of your writing rut. To do things right, you'll need to make sure you do the following. Revisit your original topic idea and make sure you have clarity on the desired outcome. Make sure you have a lot of creative space like a whiteboard or a table with sticky notes where you can visually create your mind map. The subject title should be the mind map title to remind you of what you are brainstorming. Add branches and topics and the sub-branches with their sub-topics without worrying about organization or flow for now. The organization comes later. Let all the ideas flow freely from your mind, and please take a break when you run out of ideas or struggle to concentrate. But always keep coming back to it after the short breaks until you feel like you've collected all of your thoughts. To make this even more practical, here are a few steps you can follow:

1. Place your main topic or chapter (depending on where you feel stuck) in the center of the whiteboard or table.

2. Close your eyes, take a deep breath, and summon the ideas to flow to you. Trust me, they will come to you, and as they do, I want you to jot them down on different sticky notes

as without overthinking them. If you're using a whiteboard, draw arms and label them.

3. As more details come to you, make sub-arms from the key ideas, and write short detailed notes. If using sticky notes, try to use different colored notes for the details. It helps if you can think of all the questions your reader may ask you as they go through that particular chapter or section. Keep expanding, writing whatever comes to you in no specific order until you feel complete.

4. Now you can pick up the best ideas from your mind map and structure it or group the different areas you want to talk about depending on the flow you like.

There are lots of tools available if you want to do this digitally. I prefer a big table with lots of sticky notes, but in the resources, I am going to share a free tool that I found online that seems to do the job pretty efficiently.

Self-care practices

Although we've seen a lot more emphasis placed on self-care and mindfulness practices, I think many writers still perceive it as a luxury or "only for certain people." The truth is if you inhabit a human body, you need to practice self-care.

Why is self-care an essential part of your writing success? Because with self-care comes self-compassion, both of which are integral cornerstones to improving your relationship with yourself. I have said this before, but it bears repeating. Writer's block is all real - within you. The more you learn to heal that internal conflict that creates these blocks, the more you won't have to deal with these types of obstacles. Sounds easy, right? Well, it's not.

Learning to love yourself, trust and have faith in yourself, and feel genuine compassion for yourself when things aren't going too well, is one of the most challenging tasks you'll ever face. I still struggle with it today, and I've been working at it for years now. But I'm not talking about being self-centered or selfish. On the contrary, loving yourself deepens your ability to care for others and the work you do. Self-care isn't about procrastinating or being lazy; it's about practicing self-acceptance, becoming more mindful and aware of your thoughts, behaviors, and actions. It is also about living a balanced lifestyle, which let's be honest; most writers struggle with it.

Think of it this way: it would be impossible for an architect to construct a beautiful building on a flimsy foundation. You are no different when it comes to the construction of your masterpiece. And the foundational elements needed aren't tools or external objects. What you need is a robust internal foundation that can support all that you want to produce and share with the outer world because life is an inside-out game. Now I know, this can be a daunting idea, but I encourage you to just sleep on it and reflect on the implications that have been suggested. It is more than just self-improvement or personal development. It's about learning how to deal and relate to yourself when you feel blocked or divided inside. If you are trying to increase your inspiration and creativity, why would you call upon yourself to achieve this goal, unless a part of you already has access to boundless creativity and inspiration?

It isn't a simple question to answer, and I don't expect you to, but I do want you to start shifting perspective and get more curious. As writers, curiosity comes naturally to us. Let us use this curiousness to overcome challenges such as writer's block.

Some cool new things you can try out if you want to dive into this world of self-care and self-compassion as a strategy to overcome blocks include:

Meditation

It is one of the most natural, most accessible spiritual practices that anyone can begin. I swear by meditation and honestly believe my blocks have almost become non-recurring thanks to my commitment to meditate daily. It wasn't easy when I started. I didn't know if I was doing it right, couldn't stop thoughts from distracting me, etc.

but I kept at it. Things are much better now, mainly because I stopped trying to eliminate my thoughts and started focusing on observing them instead. Experts say meditation can restructure your brain, reduce stress, give you clarity, boost immunity, and so many other amazing benefits. I'm still a novice and have much to learn, but I can already attest to the fact that something special happens when you start meditation. The demons in my head seem to be mellowing down a lot giving me enough room to focus on my craft.

Deep breathing techniques

Most of us aren't aware of the way we breathe, but in general, there are two types of breathing patterns: Thoracic, also known as chest breathing, and diaphragmatic, also known as abdominal breathing. The more anxious we become, the shallower our breathing gets, which usually means we are breathing from the chest. It causes an upset in the oxygen and carbon dioxide levels resulting in increased heart rate, muscle tension, and other physical sensations.

As you can imagine, when the blood isn't adequately circulating oxygen, the body gets stressed, which only amplifies the "blocked" state we're trying to overcome. So, a great practice to get into, especially when attempting to start writing, is to do some simple abdominal breathing exercises to connect your body, mind, and spirit. Here's something cool you can try.

Inhale slowly and deeply through your nose. Keep your shoulders relaxed. Let your abdomen expand and make sure your chest rises only a little. Then, exhale slowly through your mouth. As you blow out air, purse your lips slightly, but keep your jaw relaxed as you exhale until all the air is out. Repeat this breathing exercise for several minutes. Although you can do this exercise in any position, I recommend standing up or lying down for a more luxurious experience. Remember to focus on calming your mind or reconnecting your whole being (not thinking about how you can't think of what to write).

Yoga

Yoga can help you harmonize your body, mind, and spirit and individualized explicitly according to what your needs are at the time. There are many well-known physical benefits for doing Yoga, but there's more to it than just getting a nice workout. Yoga will help you connect with your body and the emotions that are stored deep within. It encourages non-judgment and self-acceptance about where you are in life, and we all know this is key to overcoming blocks and moving forward. There are many types of yoga, so just do a bit of exploration and try a few classes out to see what feels right for you.

Spending time in nature

The sound of birds, the warmth of the sun, the sight of trees swaying in the wind, or waves crashing on the shore make your senses come alive and can be just what you need to rekindle your creative fire. Nature always brings healing and presents moment awareness, so take time as often as you can to be in nature, even when you're not going through writer's block.

Forgiving yourself

Often, the block sticks around longer than is necessary because you get in this vicious cycle of being angry with yourself for not writing or meeting your daily writing goal, which makes you feel worse and keeps you in the same state. When you are unable to practice self-compassion and forgiveness, a lot of energy goes to waste. That's where practicing forgiveness comes in. It's essential to stay present and accept that life is about ebb and flow. Pleasure and pain are part of your journey, and overcoming challenges is part of the mastery process. Of course, the ego prefers joy and comfort, and it's a lot easier to feel good and stay present when creativity and inspiration overflow. But the discipline gained from working through stumbling blocks as you master your craft is just as relevant and helps solidify your success. The more you understand who you are and why writing is important to you, the easier it will be to practice self-forgiveness and show yourself some compassion when you stumble.

These ideas might seem a bit too far-fetched for you, so don't test all these ideas out at once. Start small, pick one practice, and, if it feels good, keep doing it until it forms into a habit. Then select and experiment with a new one. Practicing self-care will help nurture you as a whole being and leave no areas of your life unattended. It will restore calmness and confidence in your life, which is precisely what your mind needs to start cranking out words that will keep people glued to your book.

CHAPTER 7

The Secret Sauce for Finishing Your Book

Strategies that help you manage your energy, mood, focus, and productivity are all well and good. But at the end of the day, if you want to be a great writer, you're going to need something extra. You need to master your craft. It can only come from investing a ton of time writing.

Think of Ernest Hemingway, Stephen King, Lee Child, Arthur Conan Doyle, J.K. Rowling, and so many other great writers in the past or present. The most successful writers, regardless of genre or writing style, all have one thing in common - they don't just throw words on paper whenever they feel like it. If they did, they wouldn't have become great writers.

Did you know Hemingway always wrote in the morning as soon as the sun rose? Did you know Stephen King writes 2,000 words a day, rain or shine? Here are a few more fun facts that might help you see the commitment needed to make you a great writer.

Ernest Hemingway would stick to writing about 500 words a day. Michael Crichton wrote several novels that turned into films such as Jurassic Park (which I bet you recognize). His daily word count was 10,000 words. Now that's ambitious. Kate DiCamillo is an American writer of children's fiction who set her daily goal as writing two pages a day, five days a week. It translates to about 600-900 words a day. Lee Child, a British author, is best known for his Jack Reacher novels that became films starring Tom Cruise. He has a daily goal of 1,800 words and likes to write in the afternoon, from about 12 until 6 or 7 pm.

As you can see, there is no one-size-fits-all when it comes to writing goals. There is one thing these established authors have in common; they have successfully developed a secret sauce - a writing system that works for them.

So, what is the secret sauce to finishing your book and eliminating writer's block? Develop and hone your writing system. Instead of looking for tricks and loopholes, focus on building and sticking to a productive writing system. So, let's break them into steps that are easy to follow.

STEP ONE > Collecting material

Every writer needs resources and writing material. It's your job to know what you need and where to get it before you start writing.

Here are a few places you can start mining for resources:

Research

Research on relevant forums, social media threads, and other online spaces where your ideal audience naturally hangs out to speak on the topic you're writing.

Your life history

Summon your memory and read through your old journals or photo albums for ideas.

Other people's life histories

Talk to your relatives and friends. Remember to ask high-quality questions and then listen. Your ability to listen with your head and heart will help you acquire lots of material because people love to talk about themselves.

Read books and articles

Get an audible account and subscribe to relevant podcasts. And I mean a lot of them.

Follow other writers

Observe what they are doing and try to get inspiration from them. Don't copy. Just let their ideas trigger your own.

STEP TWO > Writing

Collecting your resources and material is excellent, but none of that matters if you don't sit and write. So how do you do this? Well, aside from the obvious - literally sitting down and typing or writing by hand, there are a few other things you need to help shape this new system.

Set daily goals or daily milestones

Take the examples I shared above of different writers with their daily page or word count. You need to do the same for your writing system to work. The daily milestones help move you forward toward the achievement of the bigger goals.

Choose a start time

Some people want to write with the sunrise, and others want to write in the middle of the night. Choose a time that works for you and feels most productive then stick to it.

Create a deliberate constriction

In other words, choose to limit yourself. Bestselling novelist Jodi Picoult once said, "writer's block is having too much time on your hands. If you have a limited amount of time to write, you just sit down and do it."

STEP THREE > Honing your craft

As with any other type of mastery, if you want to become great, you must take time to work on your craft. And like any other craft, there are best practices and recognized levels of proficiency. There are so many things you can do to keep improving your art, but you must be proactive. Some people prefer to hire a writing coach or purchase a writing course to help improve their work. Others want the self-taught route, which is excellent too. So, here are a few suggestions that I've found useful.

Read a book on writing

I recommend Stephen King's book titled "On Writing" and Anne Lamott's " Bird by Bird." You can also check out blogs like ProBlogger (Darren Hardy owns this blog where lots of useful information is shared).

Dissect specific aspects of writing that you enjoy and aspire to do

It is where practicing mindful reading takes effect. It's not enough to just read; you also need to pay attention to how the author made the book remarkable.

Here's a practical exercise you can do immediately to hone your craft and stir up your creativity simultaneously.

Go to Amazon, select the category you are writing for in the Kindle Books section, and pick the Best Sellers that catch your eye. Now do a little more digging by going into the sub-category you're writing in and collect a sample size of at least five books out of the top ten. Be meticulous in choosing those top five then read all samples.

Here's a question you want to answer when done reading. Did the first line hook me? If yes, why? If no, why not? And if you did get hooked, how did the author manage to do it? You also want to take note of the books that made you want to keep reading and ask yourself what the author did to stimulate that urge in you. Could you already figure out the viewpoint of the main character? How did you feel about him or her? Why were you able to connect with the character so much?

Now that you've done this practical exercise, it's time to reflect on your work in progress. Are there elements you can incorporate into your book as well? What new ideas are coming up? And just like that, you're back in the original game.

Conduct an in-depth analysis of a book or a blog

All good writers create stories that are well organized and understandable, so when analyzing a book, here are a few pointers. Start with the characters. Get to know who the main characters are, their biases, what their roles are in the unfolding of the story, etc. Then carefully look at the events, what happens in the story, and ask yourself why the events play out as they do. Can you easily figure out the theme, setting, and whether any symbolism has been used? How is the story organized? What is the writing style of the author? Is the writing richly detailed or sparse? Be sure to take lots of notes as you go through this exercise.

How I Recommend Putting all this Together

I know it can be daunting (after gathering all this knowledge), knowing how to make it work for you. So, here's an overview of how I've developed my writing system keeping in mind that it's still work in progress too.

Researching and assembling my materials

On average, I am reading three books on various topics at any given moment. I also research online for comments and articles around the given topic I want to write. I read first thing in the morning and also make it a priority to read the last thing at night.

As I find interesting ideas, I highlight them or use my Evernote if it's online. Here's where I like to mine for gold when it comes to my writing.

1. I subscribe to multiple writers' email lists and also have a list that I continue to update of authors or books I want to read.

2. As I do the dishes every evening or other household duties, I am actively listening to audiobooks, podcasts, or other audio content.

When it comes to collecting all my materials in an organized place, I am a sucker for Evernote if it's online or the good old highlighter pen. I also have a notes app on my iPad, which is very handy as I can jot down notes as soon as they come to me. If I am outdoors and can't access my app, I email myself the ideas. I am also creating a swipe file folder where I am saving URLs of fascinating articles and web pages on the various topics I write.

Finally, when it comes to writing and honing my craft, I do my best to keep things super simple. I write around the same time every day, even on weekends and holidays. Currently, my daily goal is 1,000 words, but I want to work that up to 2,500 in each sitting. Music is essential to my writing. Without it, nothing of value gets accomplished. If, while writing a new and unrelated idea comes to me, I don't just ignore it. Instead, I note it down on my app so I can assess it later, and I have trained myself to stick to that writing until I reach my daily goal come what may. Most days I find that I can even continue with my story past the 1,000-word count, but I stop myself while I'm still hot because I realized (having taken the lesson from Hemmingway) that if I stop while I'm still productive, getting back into it the next day is super easy. It is how I have managed to go a long time without any writer's block. To top it off, honing my skills isn't just about the daily writing, it has also become about reading books on writing. I do my best to analyze novels from authors I like. I can assure you, however, that every writer is different in his or her approach. So, if what I'm doing doesn't feel right for you, that's perfectly fine. This book is a guideline to help you develop a system that works for you and prevents you from falling into the dreaded writer's block.

I want you to write your system following the steps I wrote and clearly state how you will gather your resources, how and when you will write, and what you will do to start developing your skills. Be as detailed as possible; print it out and hang it where you can see it until it becomes the only way you work. Of course, you may not always be able to follow the detailed document to a tee when life gives you some unexpected curveballs. But having that written document will enable you to bounce back and figure out any leaks that need fixing.

Finding a Big Enough Motive to Jump-Start Your Writing and Get You Unstuck

While we writers love what we do, no one said this path would be easy. This uphill struggle that you feel stuck in is something every writer is very familiar with, so why do we do it? What drives us to keep going even in the face of rejection, self-doubt, loneliness, and oh yes, writer's block?

If your mind wants to do anything but write and you're wondering how you will ever finish your project, this is an excellent time to take a step back and remind yourself of what keeps you passionate about your writing.

Perhaps for you, the driving factor is sharing your wisdom, knowledge, and story with the world. Maybe you have a desire to give people the benefits of the experiences you've had, the places you've been, the people you've met, and the things you've seen and done.

There's nothing more satisfying in the world than the hope that our writing has touched even a single person and made their life better. Whether it's to motivate the person to make a change, to inspire them to keep persevering and achieve goals, to help heal a broken heart, or to help a reader move on, let go, shed a tear, smile, or laugh out loud. The fact that we can produce words that people can relate to at that deeper level is one of the most significant driving factors behind most writers, including myself. So, what is truly driving you to write this book? Surely if you can honestly answer that question within yourself, the next steps and your new words typed out shall begin to take form in your mind. Whether you now realize this fully or not, the same mind is lost for words; it's the same mind that holds the finished blueprint of your book. Seek no further than your own mind to help find the words needed to reach your goal successfully.

CONCLUSION

You've received encouraging words from various writers whose advice I've added in this book as well as my struggles, strategies, and systems all aimed at showing you that you can overcome writer's block. It can be very discouraging to feel stuck, but as Maya Angelou pointed out at the beginning, we must be careful not to give too much power to the realization that there's a block preventing us from doing what we love. As long as you don't give up on your writing and finishing your project, you will overcome it. Find creative ways to inspire yourself, test every tip, suggestion, and strategy outlined in this book. Keep yourself accountable, and do not forget to reconnect with your why. Remind yourself why you got into writing in the first place and why this current book needs to be finished and published.

When you finally do summon your muse and start writing again, release the past, forgive yourself, and don't feel guilty for falling behind. The lost creativity and inspiration will come back, and, as soon as it pours in, make sure you reflect to see where you can improve and the support structures you can set up to make sure you prevent this from happening in the future. Remember that writing system we touched on earlier?

Now is the time to start creating it. Put this book down, open a new document, and start building your first system for writing. It is one of the secret ingredients that will ensure your writing career gets better with time.

RESOURCES

Chapter 6, Sleep on it, page 125-126:
Tuck. "Creativity and Sleep" Jan 9, 2020,
https://www.tuck.com/creativity-and-sleep/
Jan 10, 2020.

Chapter 5, Increasing Your Productivity, page 113-114:
Deci, Edward L. "Why We Do What We Do: Understanding Self-Motivation" Aug 1, 1996,
https://www.amazon.com/Why-We-WhatUnderstanding-Self-Motivation/dp/0140255265 Jan 11, 2020.

Chapter 5, Tips on How to Manage Your Energy, page 110-111:
Chopra, Deepak. "Super Brain: Unleashing the Explosive Power of Your Mind to Maximize Health, Happiness, and Spiritual Well-Being" Nov 6, 2012, https://www.amazon.it/Super-Brain-Unleashing-Explosive-Well-Being/dp/0307956830 Jan 11, 2020

Chapter 3, Read a book on writing, page 139:
King, Stephen. "On Writing: A Memoir of the Craft" Oct 3, 2000,
https://www.amazon.co.uk/Writing-Memoir-Craft-Stephen-King/dp/1444723251
Jan 10, 2020

What Did You Think of The Writer Experience?

First of all, thank you for purchasing this book, The Writer Experience. I know you could have picked any number of books to read, but you picked this book and for that I am extremely grateful.

*I hope that it added value and quality to your writing life. If so, it would be really nice if you could share this book with your writing friends, family and community by posting to **Facebook** and **Twitter**.*

If you enjoyed this book and found some benefit in reading it, I'd like to hear from you and hope that you could take some time to post an honest review. I value my readers feedback as gaining exposure as an independent author relies mostly on word of mouth reviews and this would greatly improve my writing craft for future projects and make this book even better. So, if you have the time and inclination, it would be much appreciated.

If you'd like to leave a review, all you have to do is either use the link below or scan the QR Code and away you go.

I wish you all the best in your future success!

151

About the Author

Roger Willis is an established writing coach with the view to help people write from conception to the final manuscript. For over ten years, he is considered a trusted coach with immense knowledge. He has helped hundreds of talented writers unlock their creativity and writing skills, embrace the right mindset, and tackle writer's block; through to successfully publishing and marketing their writing crafts.

Roger lives in North Carolina, USA, with his wife and two children. He studied an MSc degree in Psychology and spent his previous working life as a Teacher before following his passion for writing and became a full-time author and coach in 2010.

He has a love for traveling with his family and reading thriller and sci-fi/fantasy books. He's an avid table tennis player and considers himself quite the wine tasting expert.

Roger has also written sci-fi and fantasy books under several pen names. He's currently writing more self-help books to help writers across the world to follow their passion and master the art of writing – watch this space.